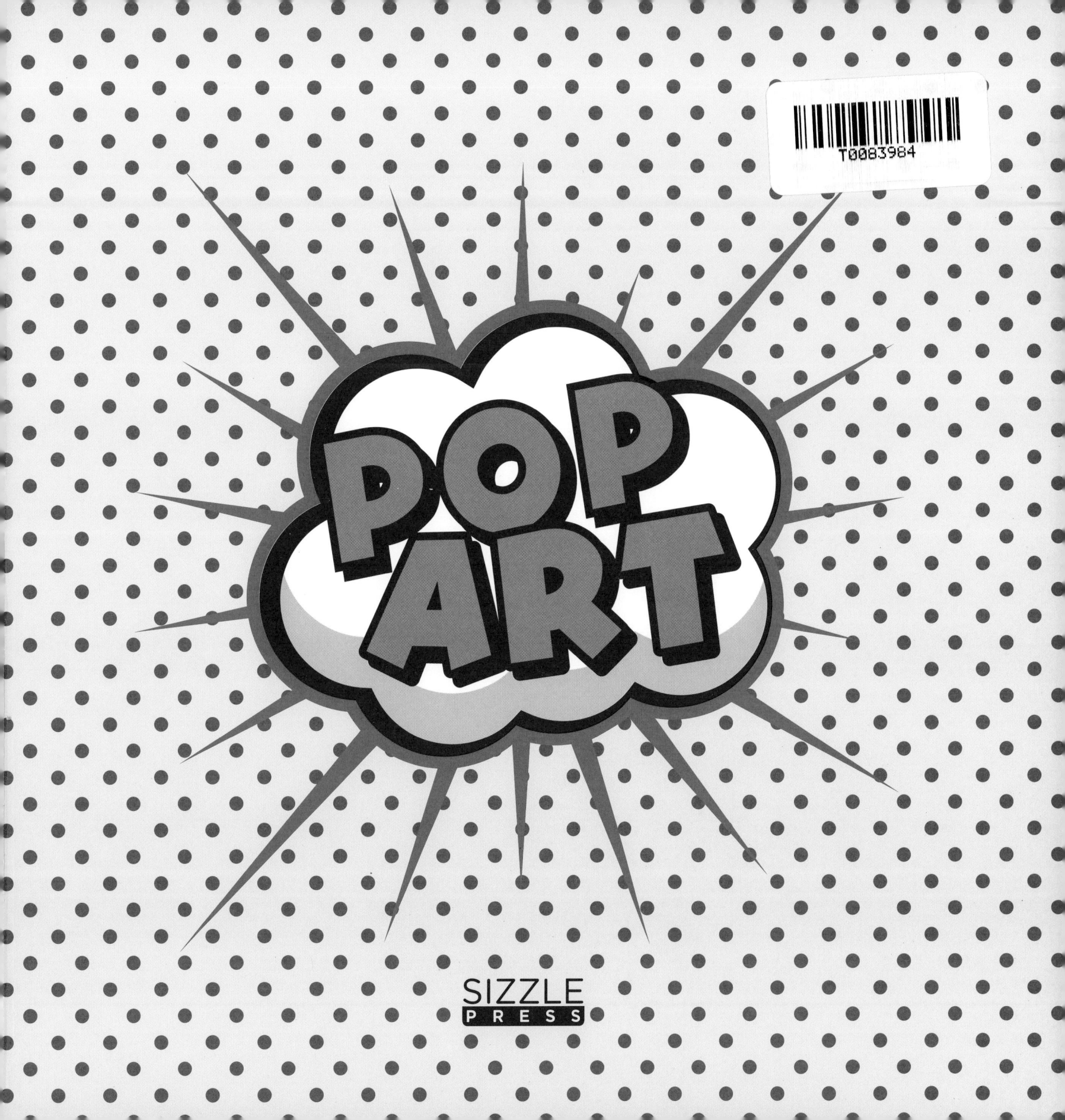
T0083984
POP ART
SIZZLE
PRESS

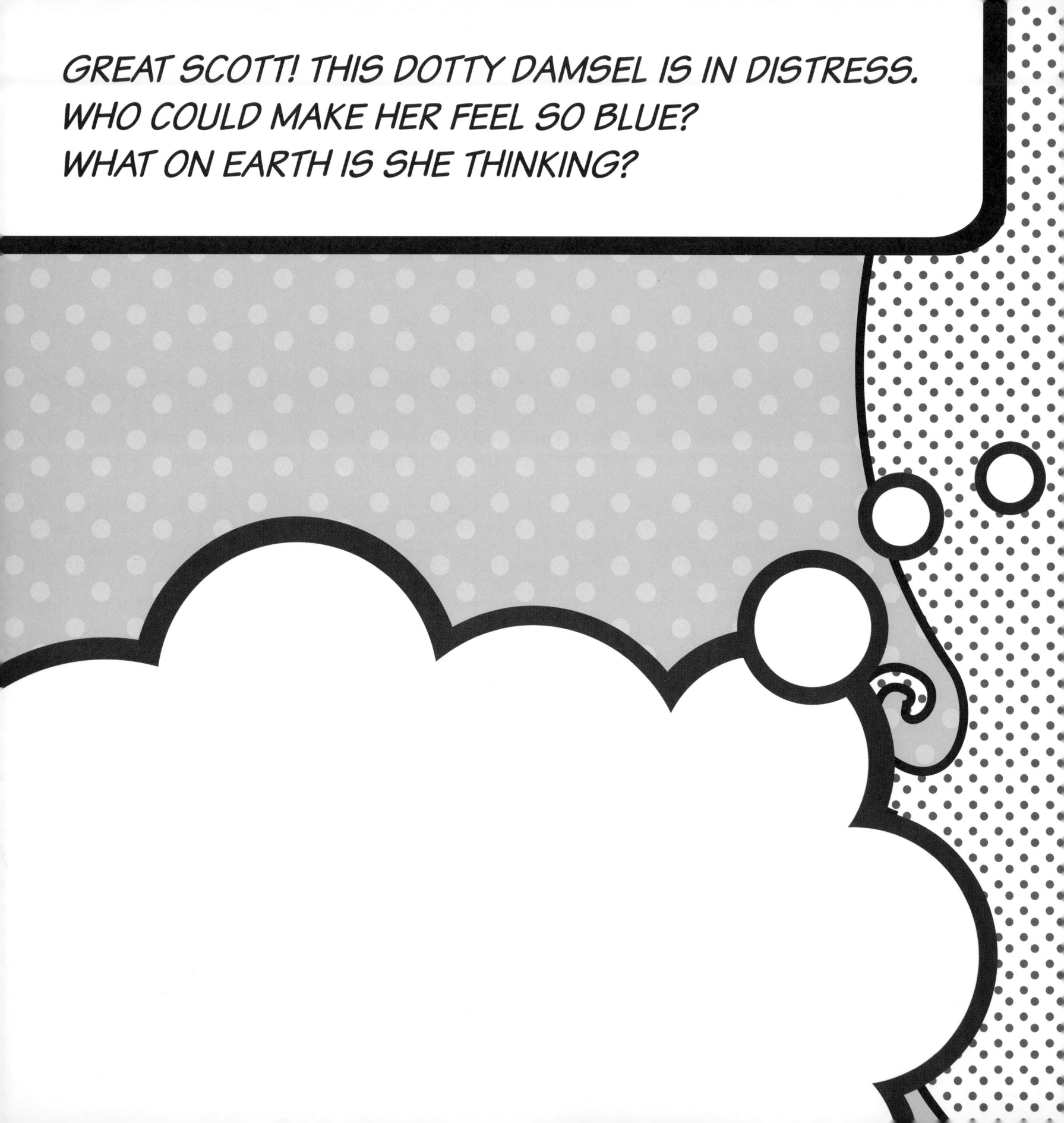
GREAT SCOTT! THIS DOTTY DAMSEL IS IN DISTRESS.
WHO COULD MAKE HER FEEL SO BLUE?
WHAT ON EARTH IS SHE THINKING?

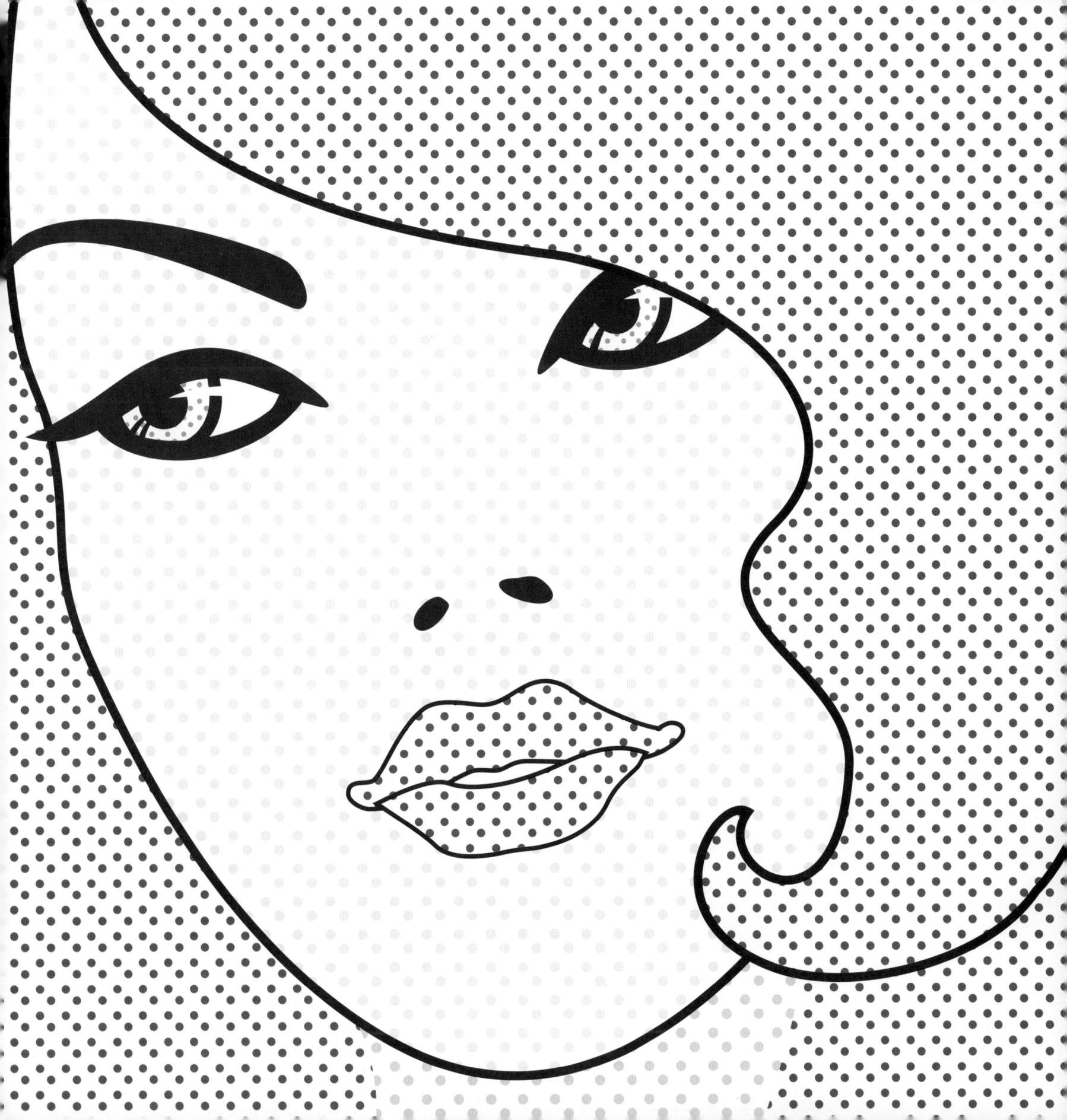

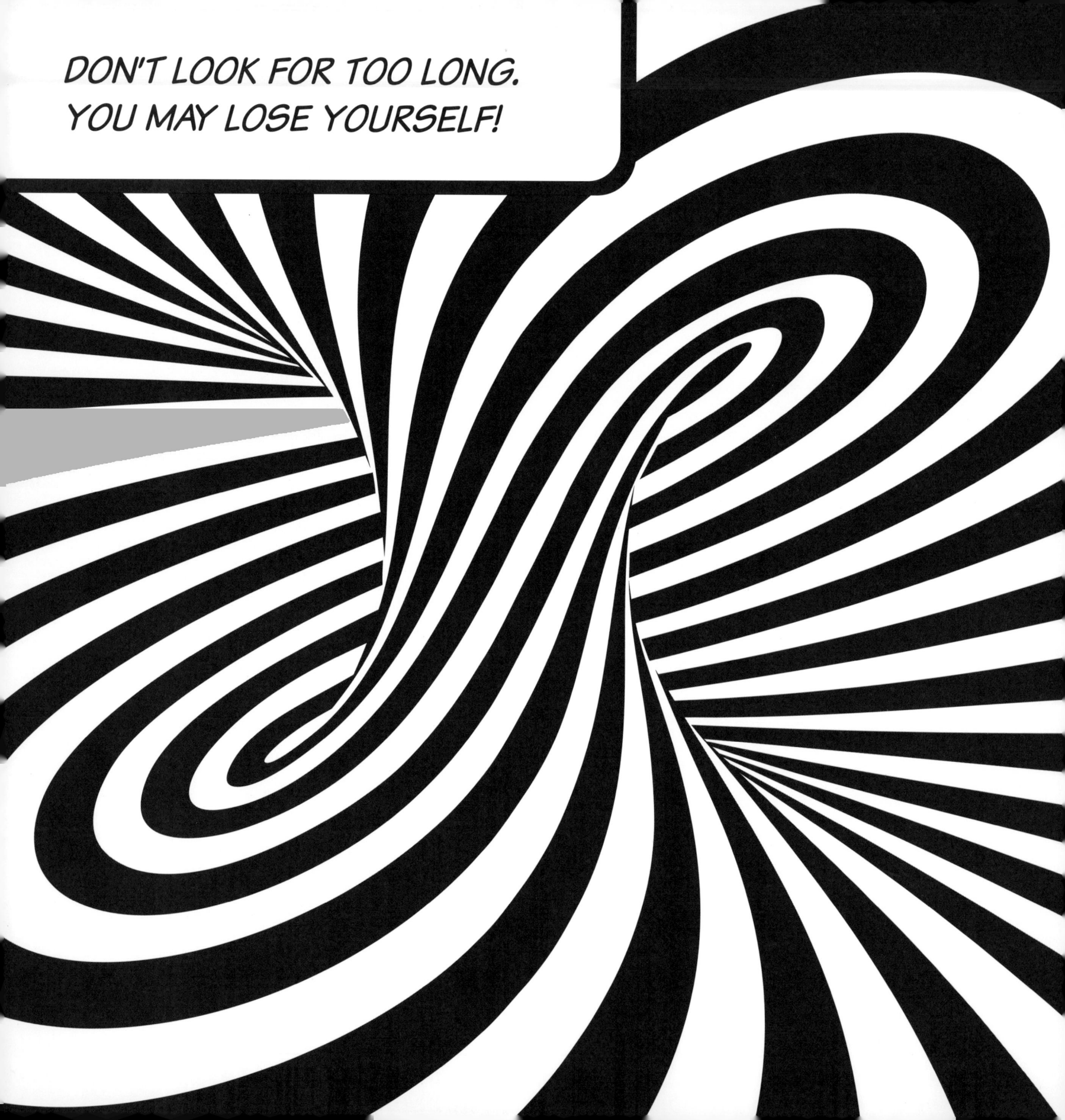
DON'T LOOK FOR TOO LONG.
YOU MAY LOSE YOURSELF!

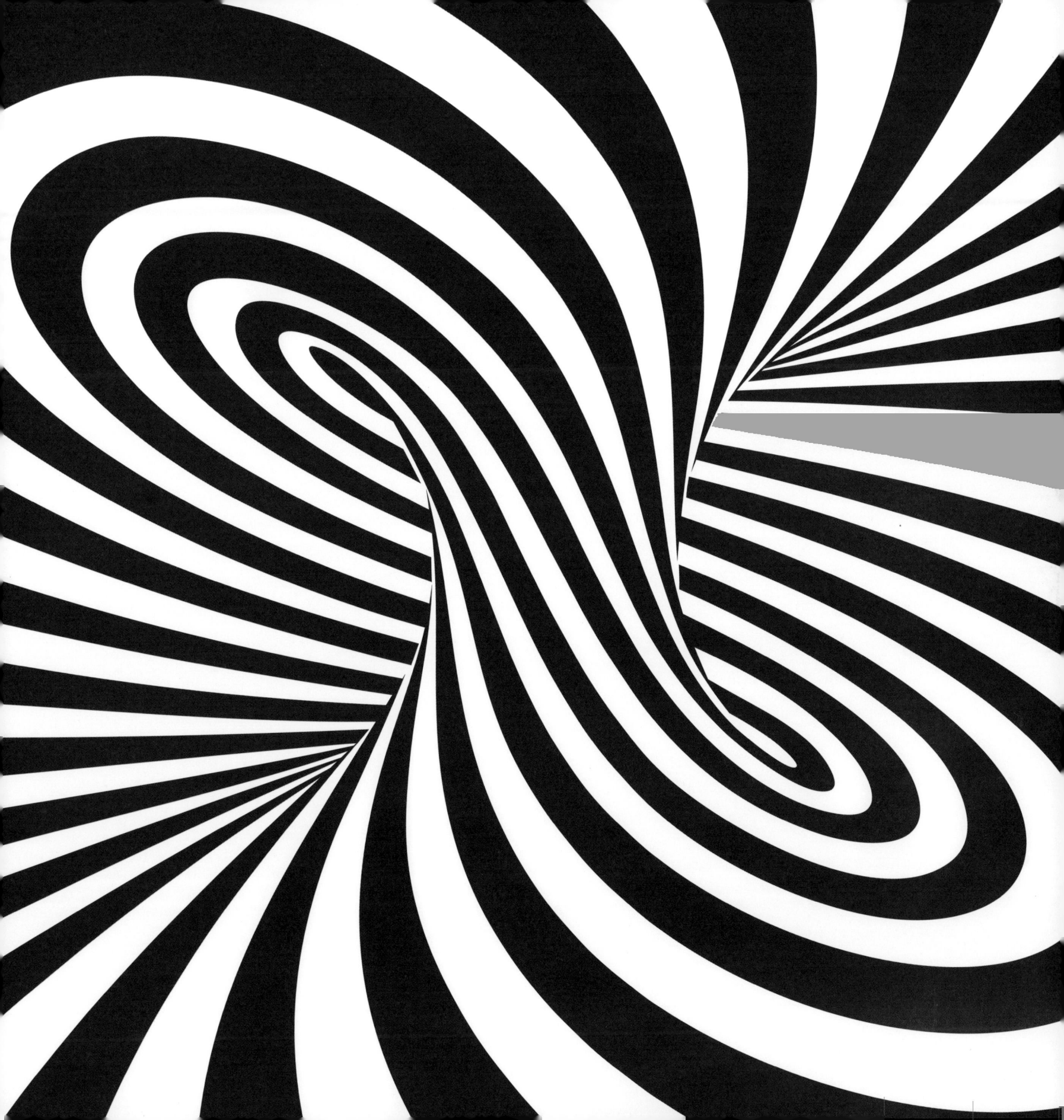

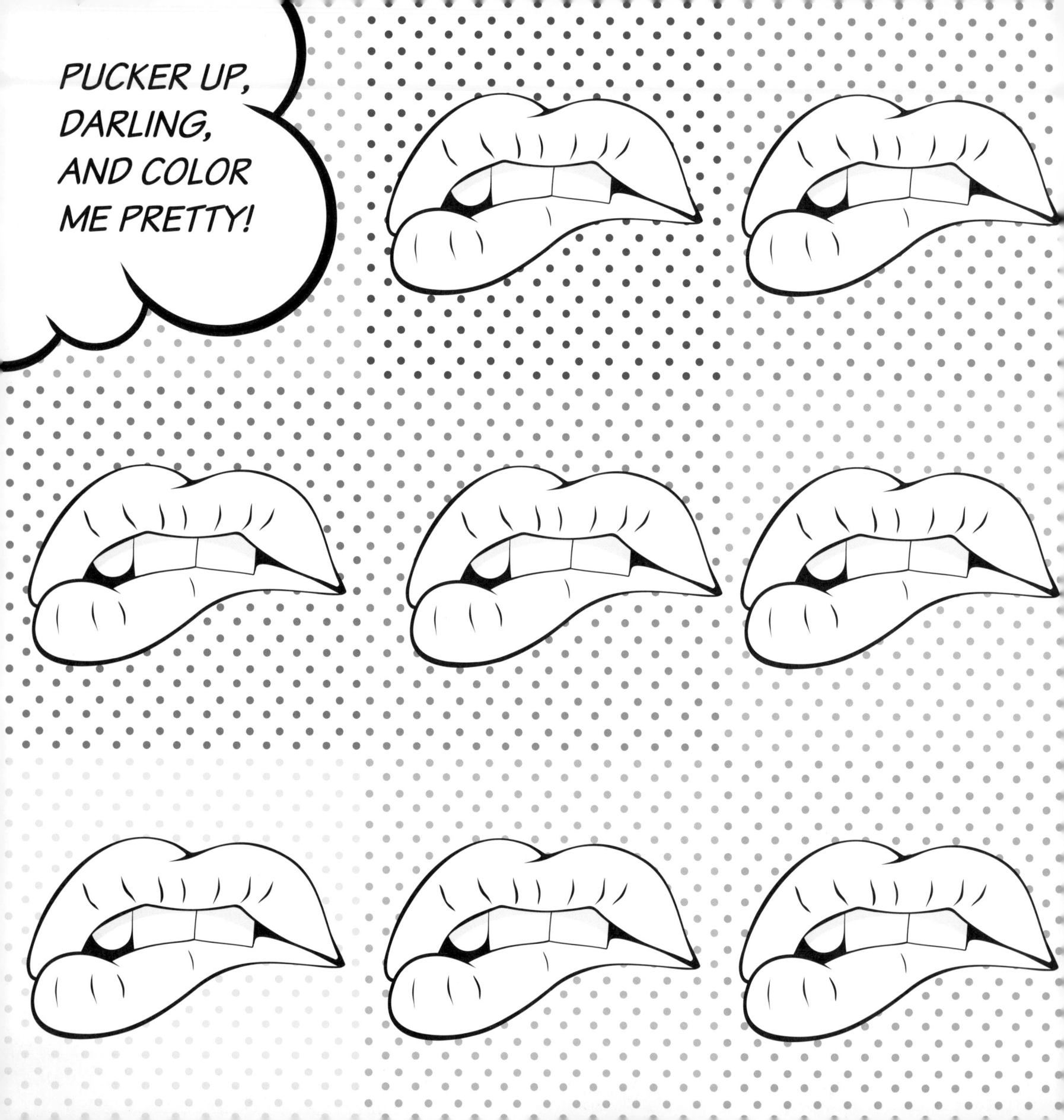
PUCKER UP, DARLING, AND COLOR ME PRETTY!

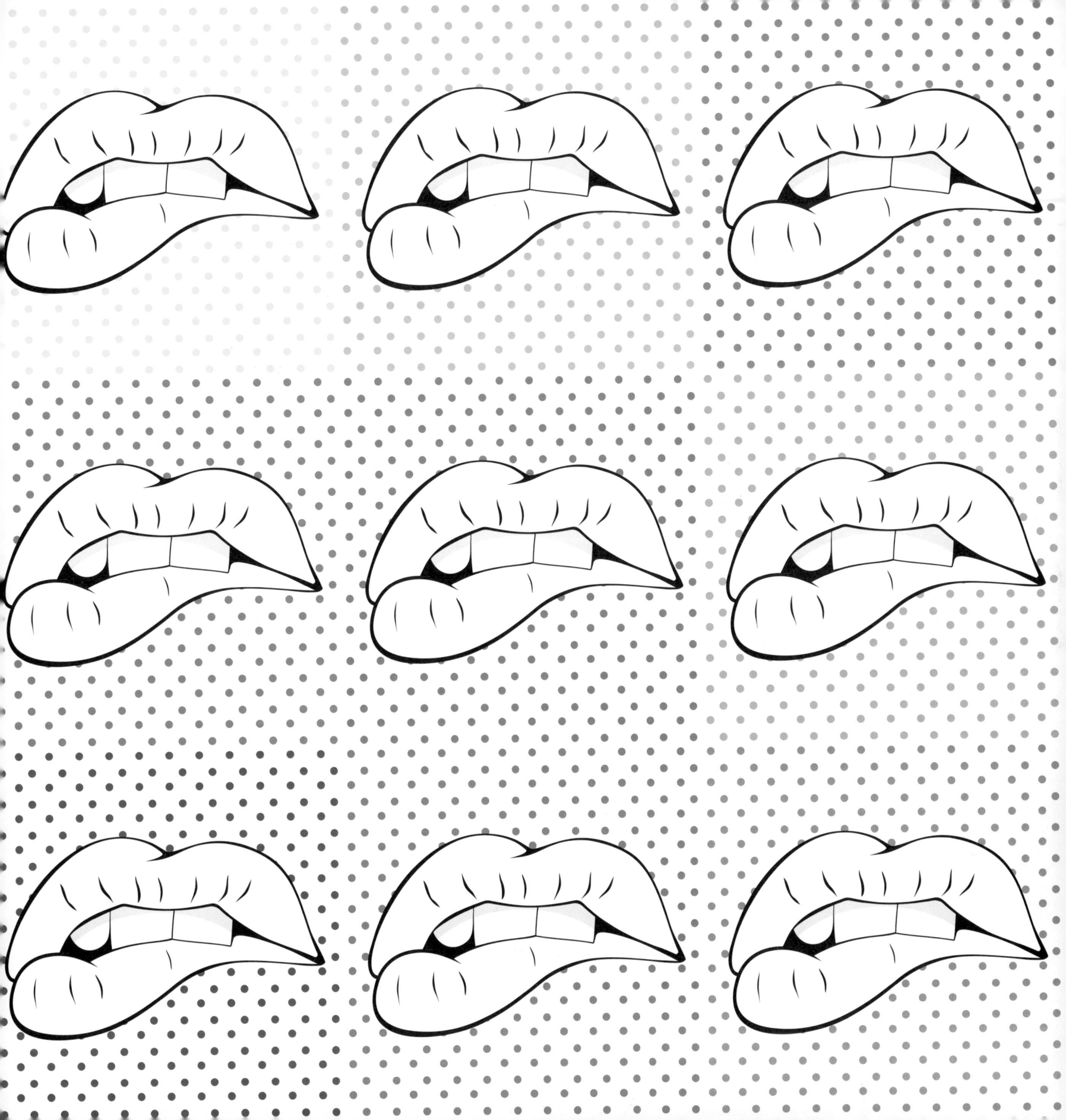

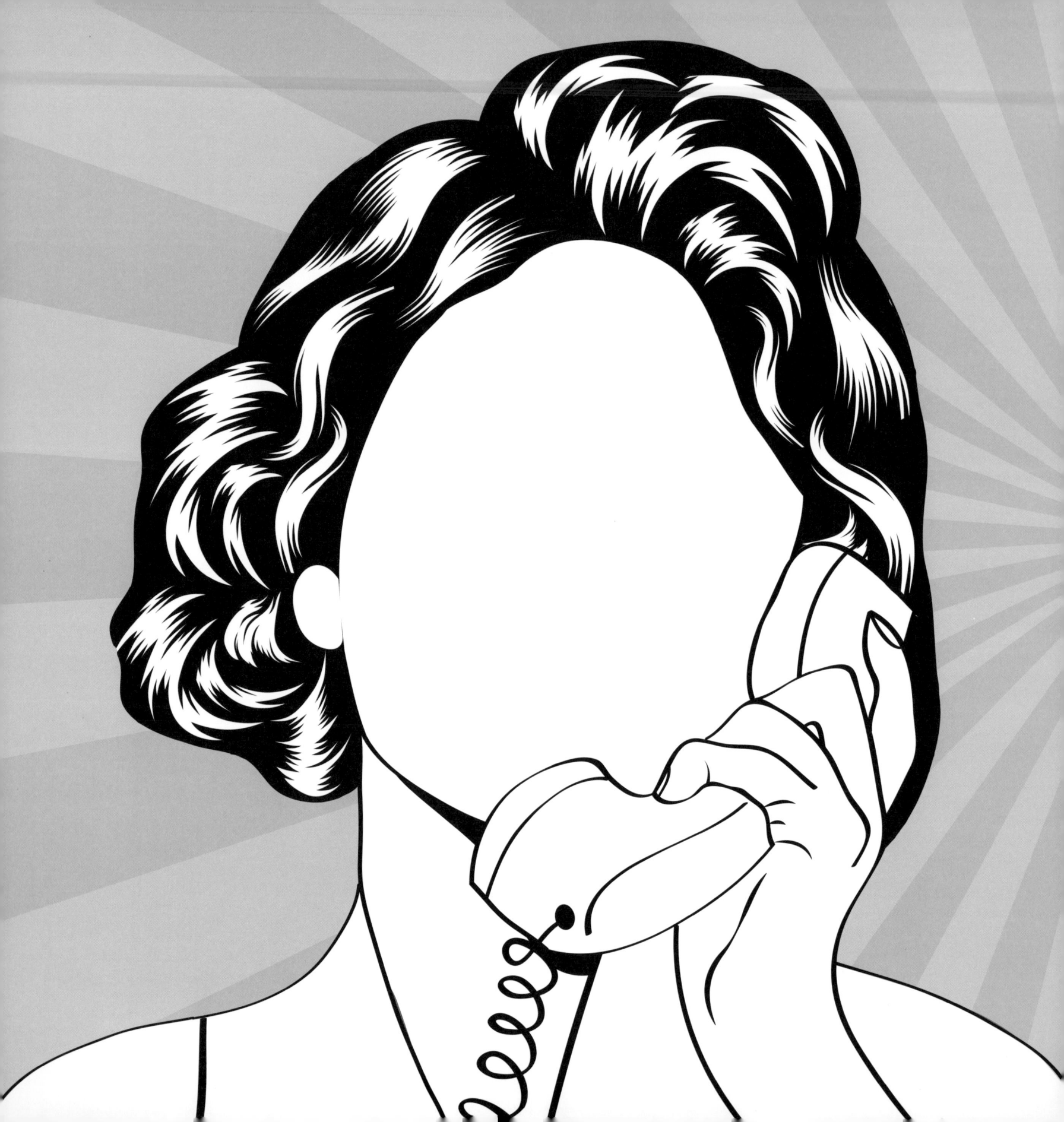

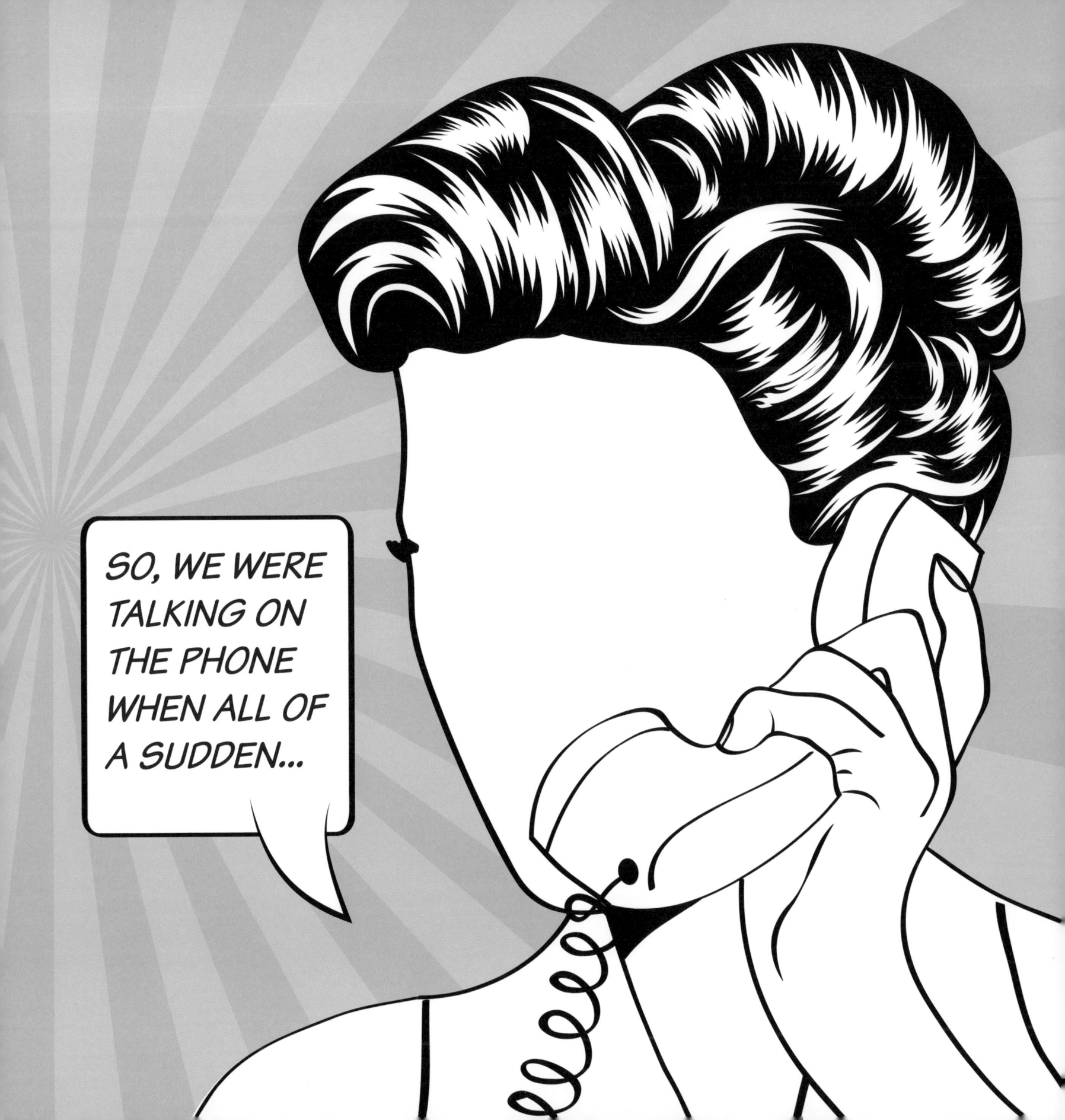
SO, WE WERE TALKING ON THE PHONE WHEN ALL OF A SUDDEN...

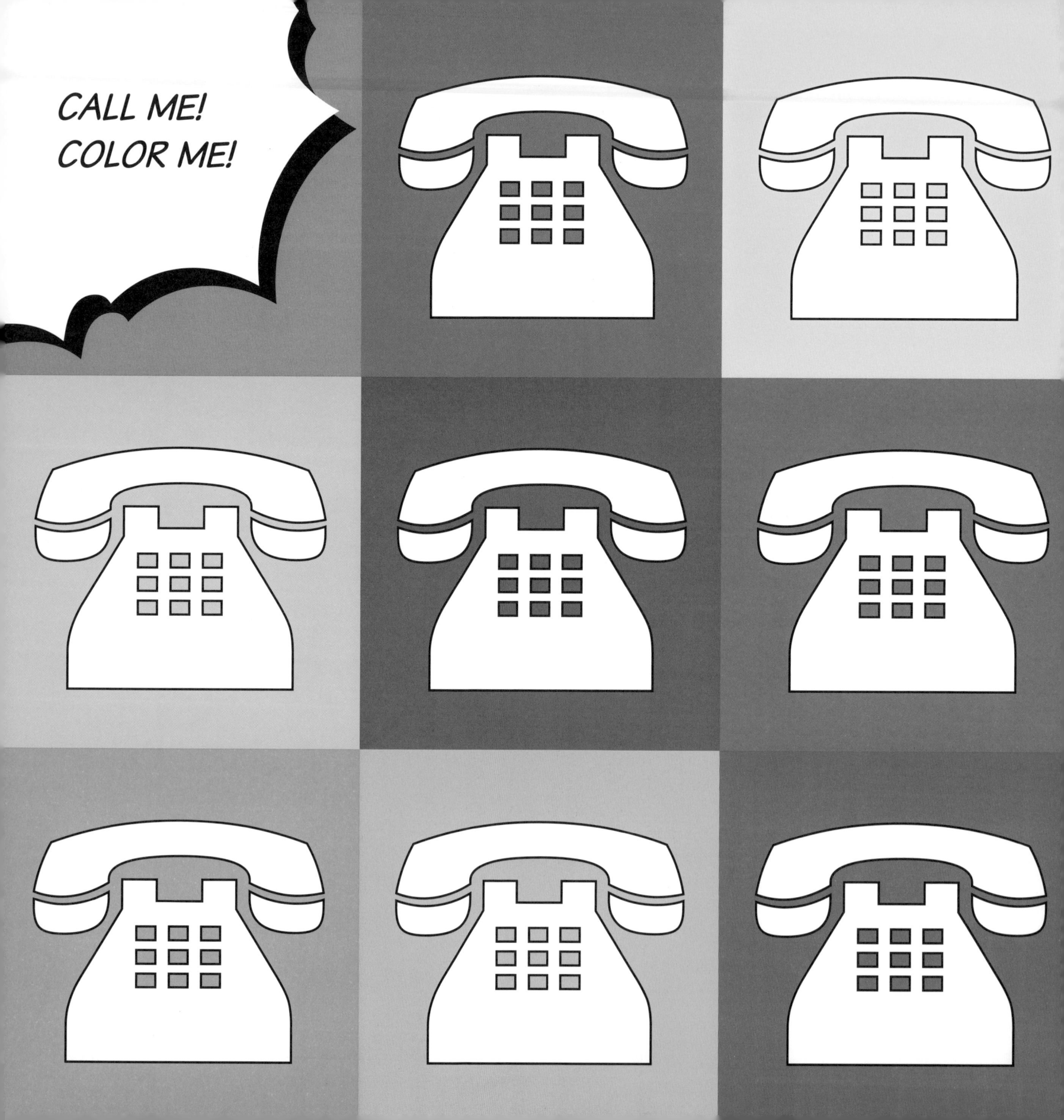
CALL ME!
COLOR ME!

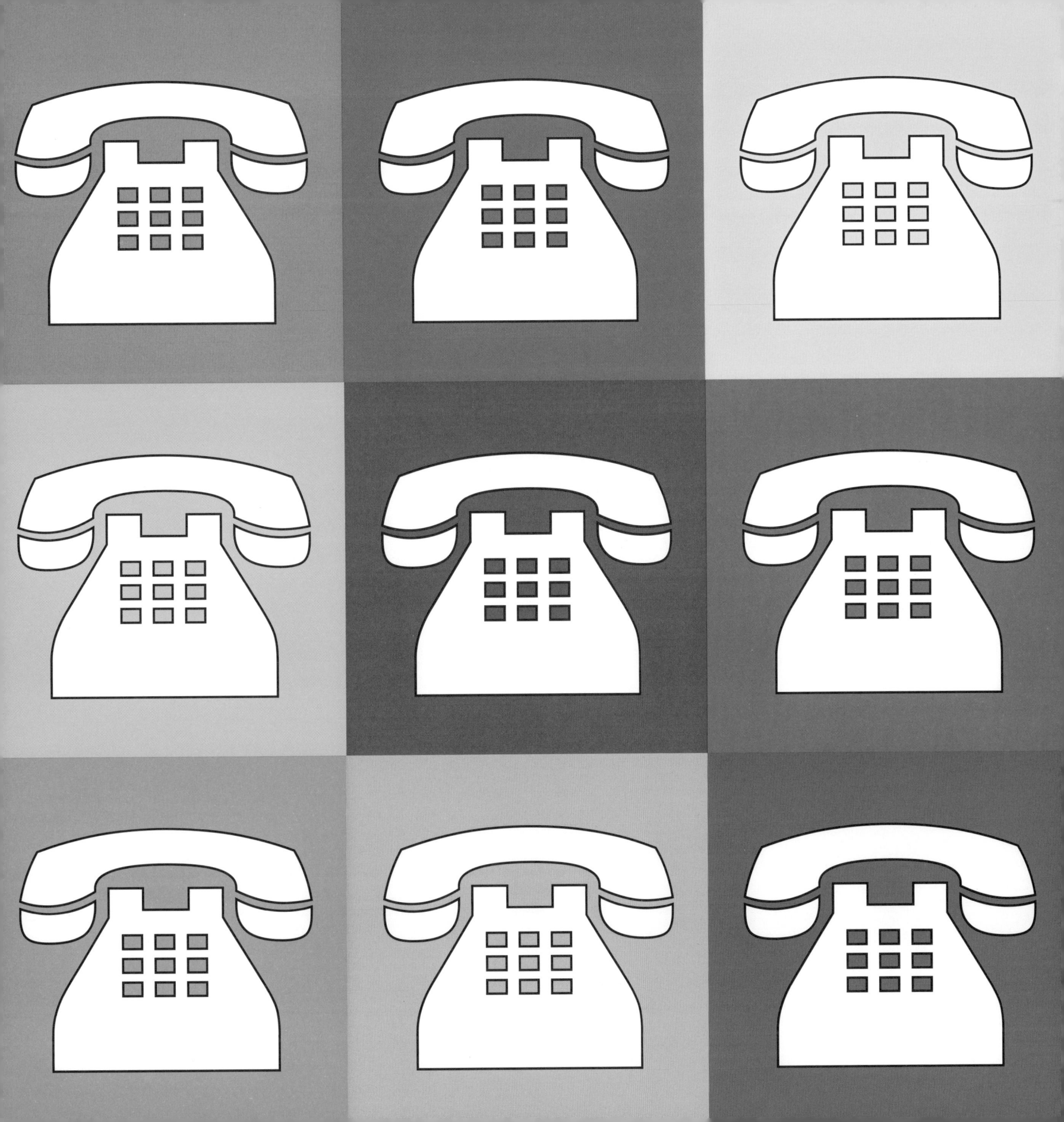

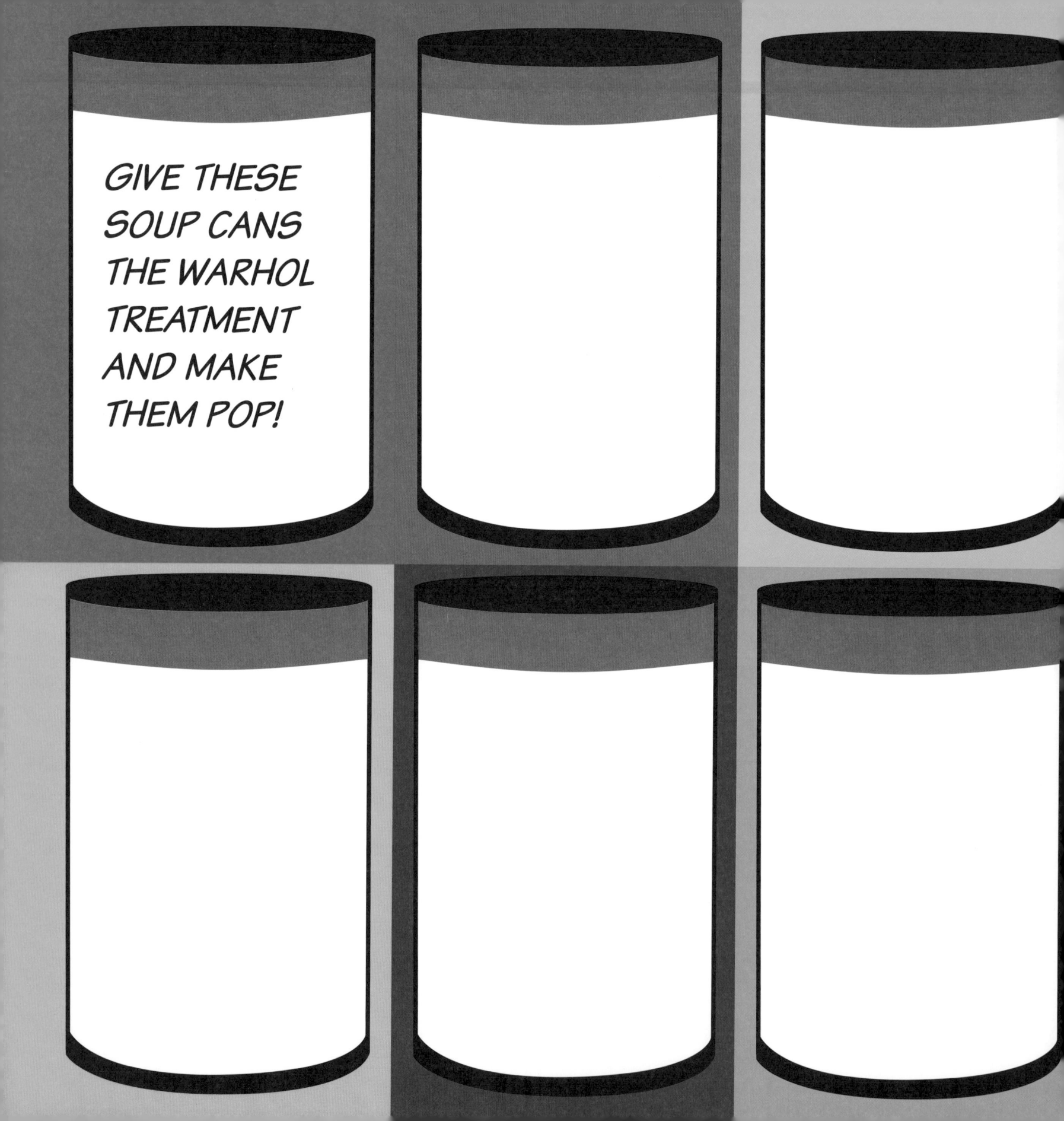
GIVE THESE SOUP CANS THE WARHOL TREATMENT AND MAKE THEM POP!

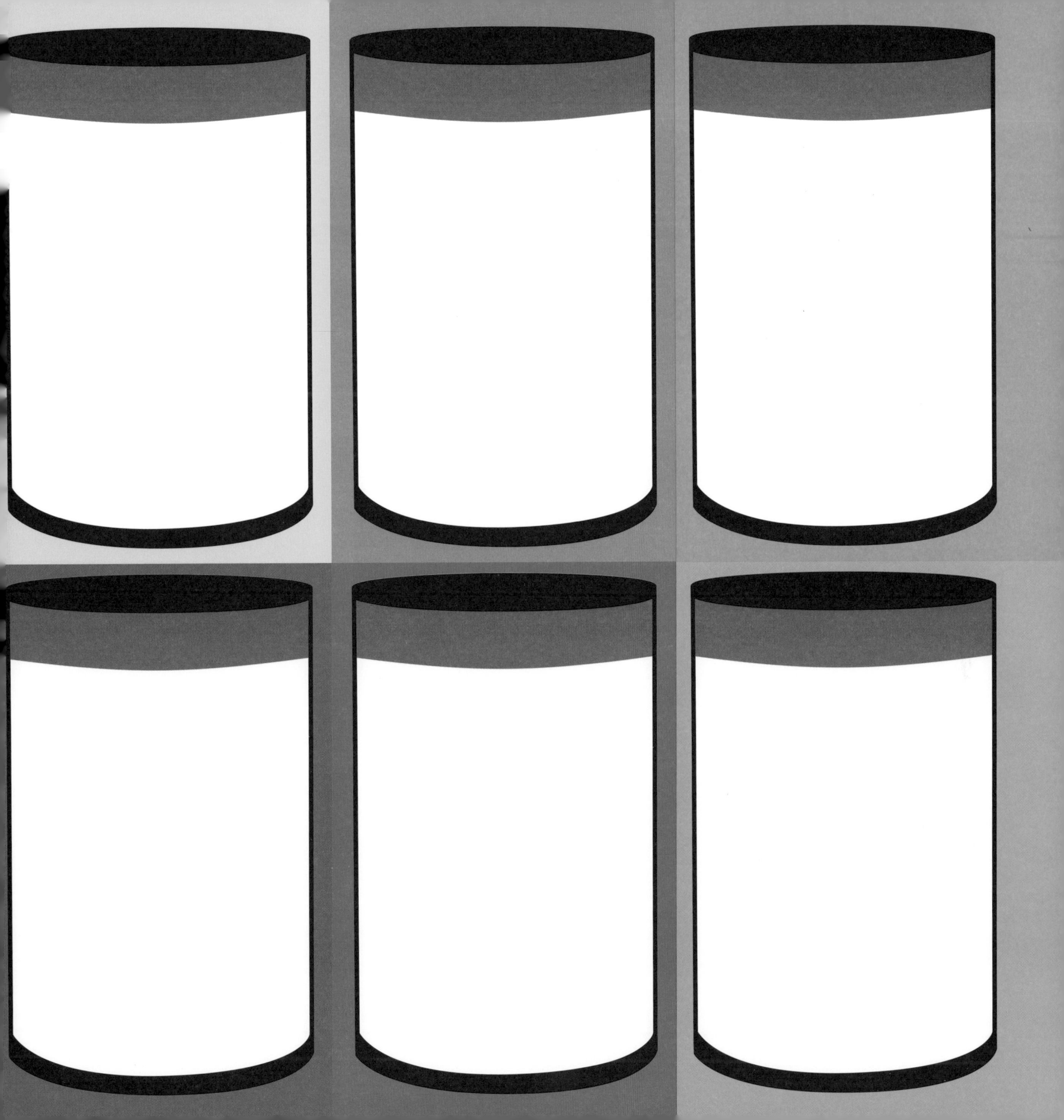

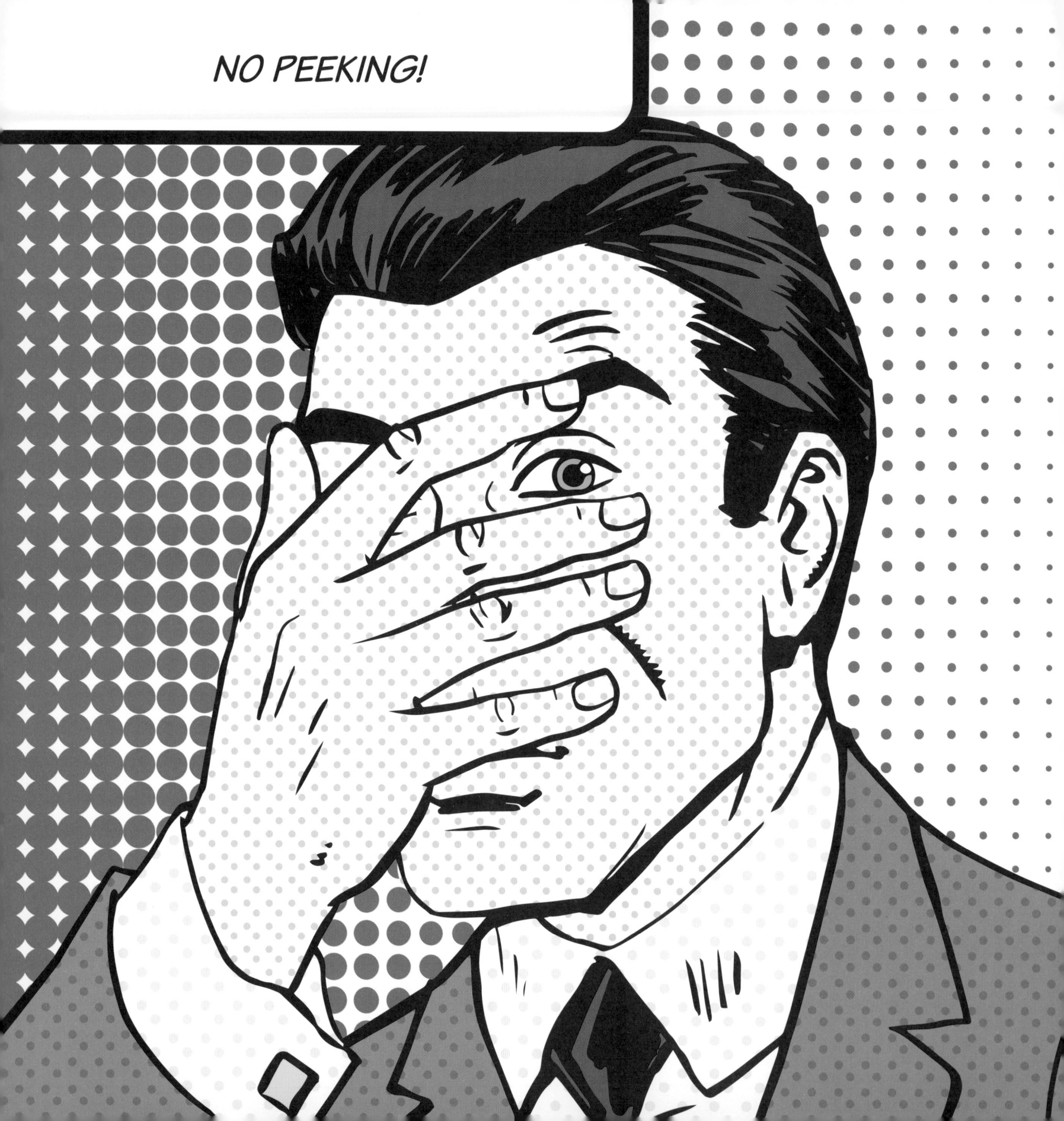
NO PEEKING!

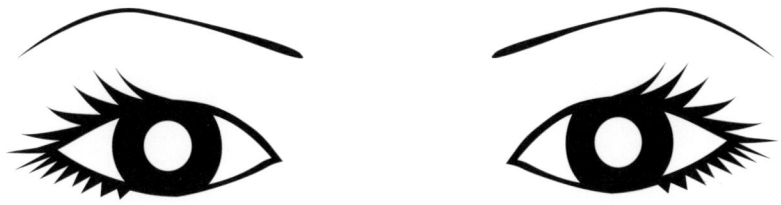

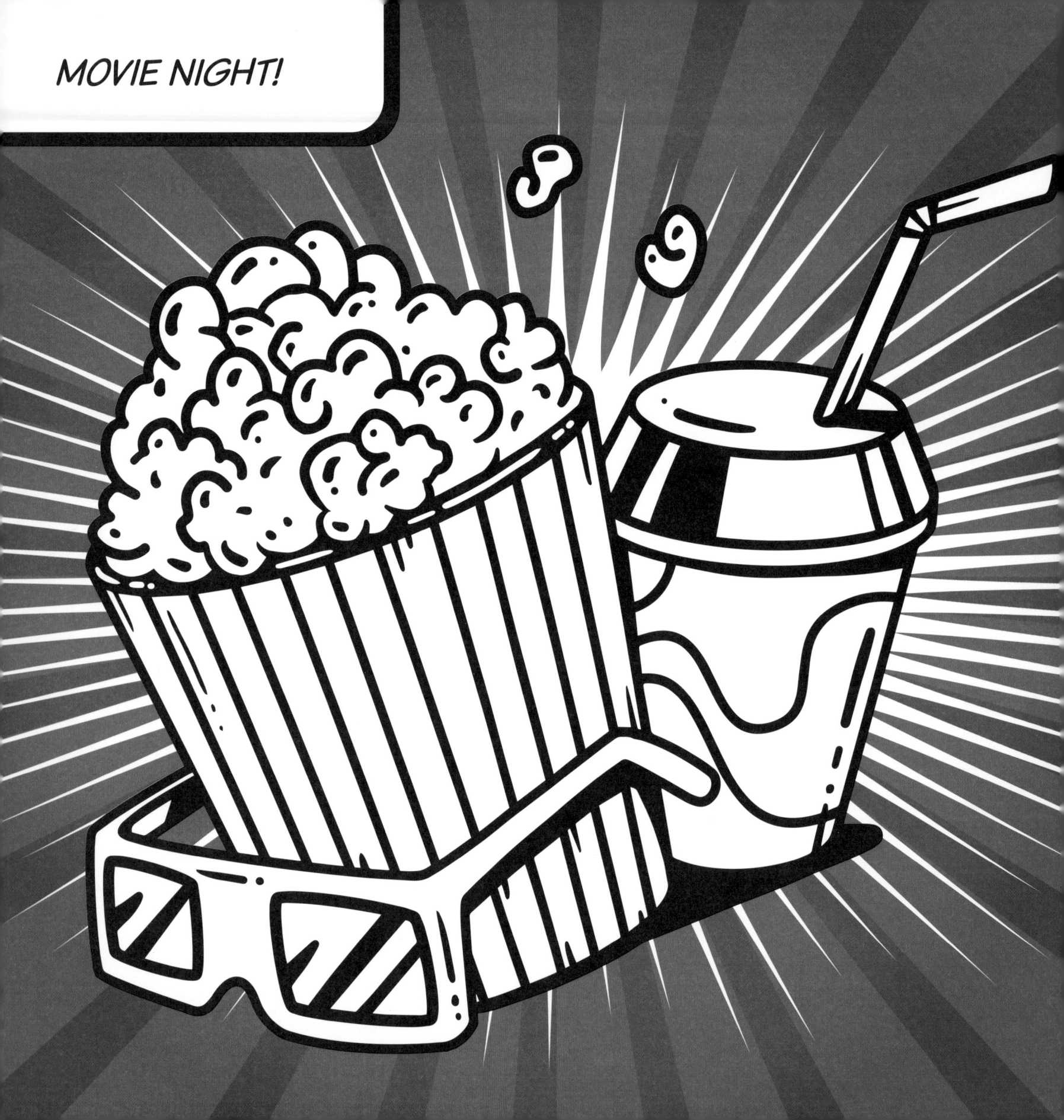
MOVIE NIGHT!

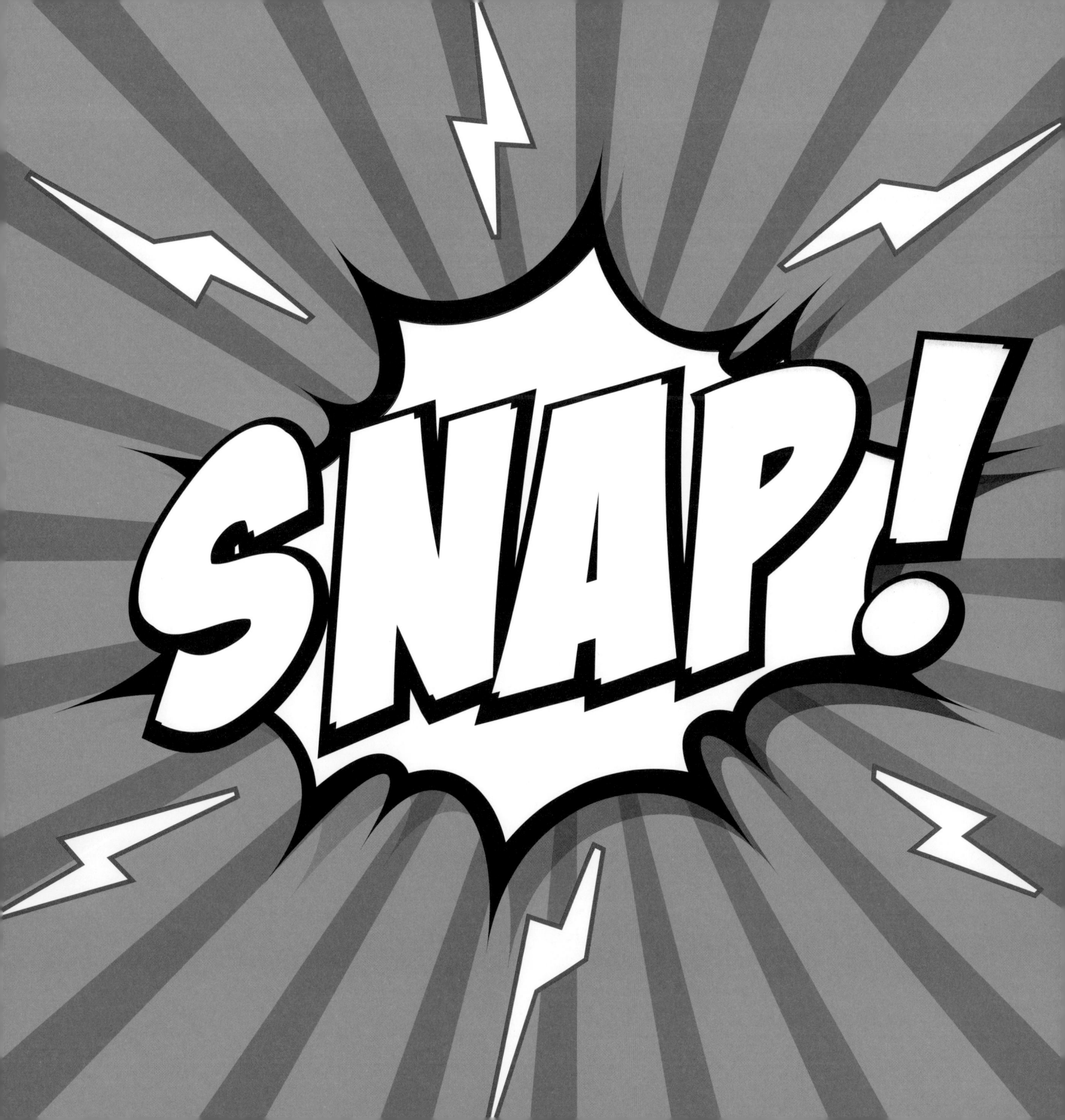
SNAP!

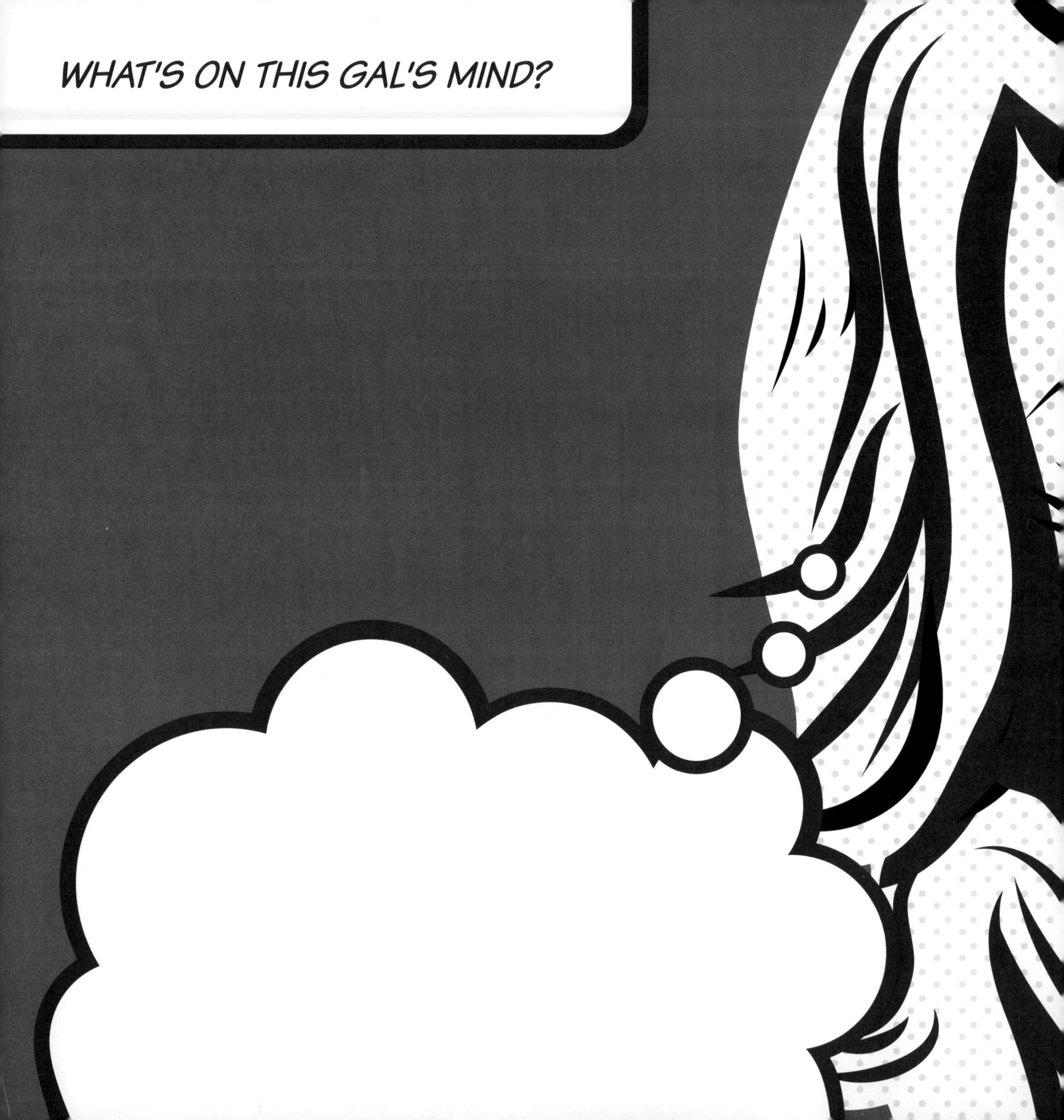
WHAT'S ON THIS GAL'S MIND?

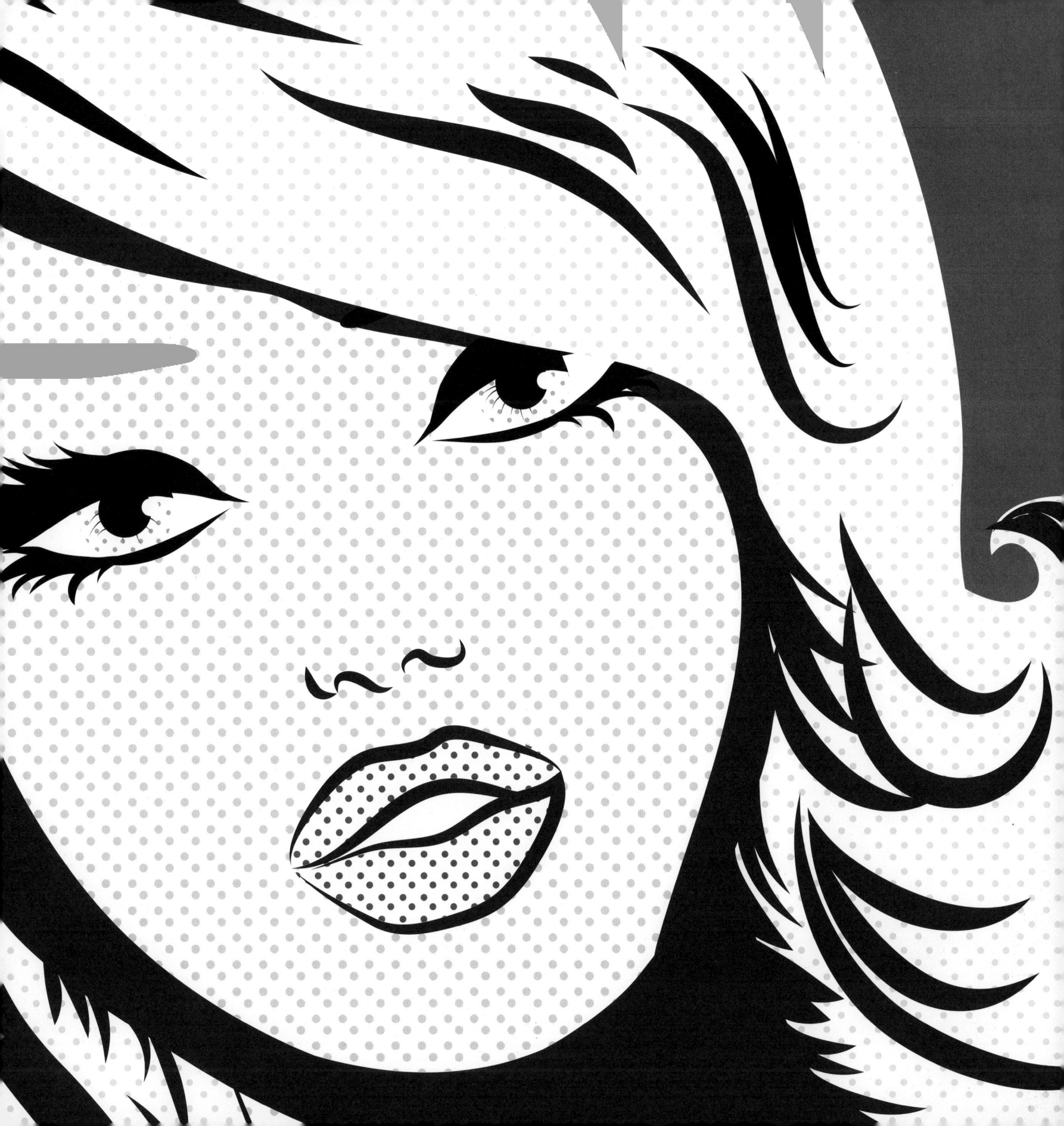

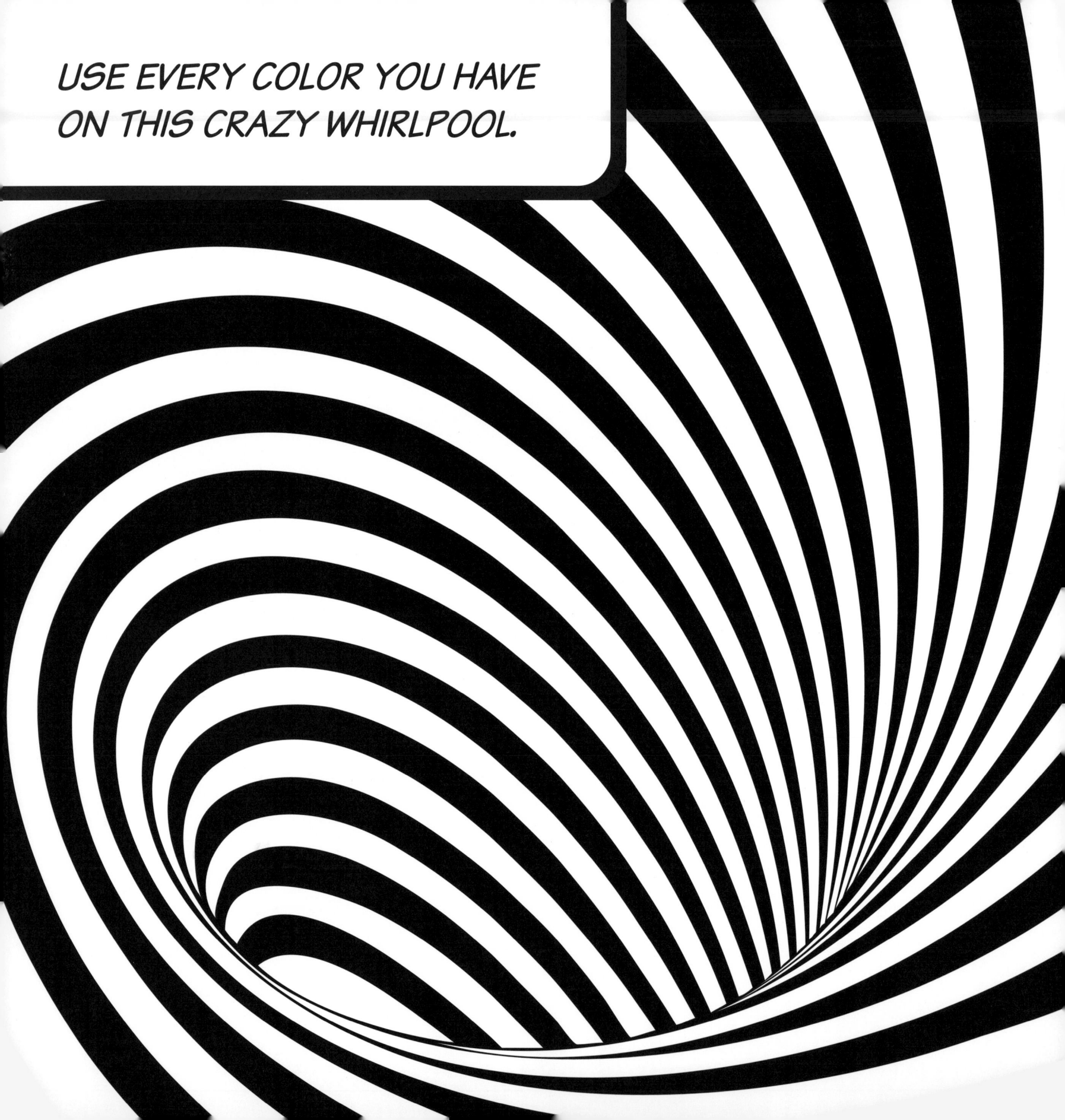
USE EVERY COLOR YOU HAVE
ON THIS CRAZY WHIRLPOOL.

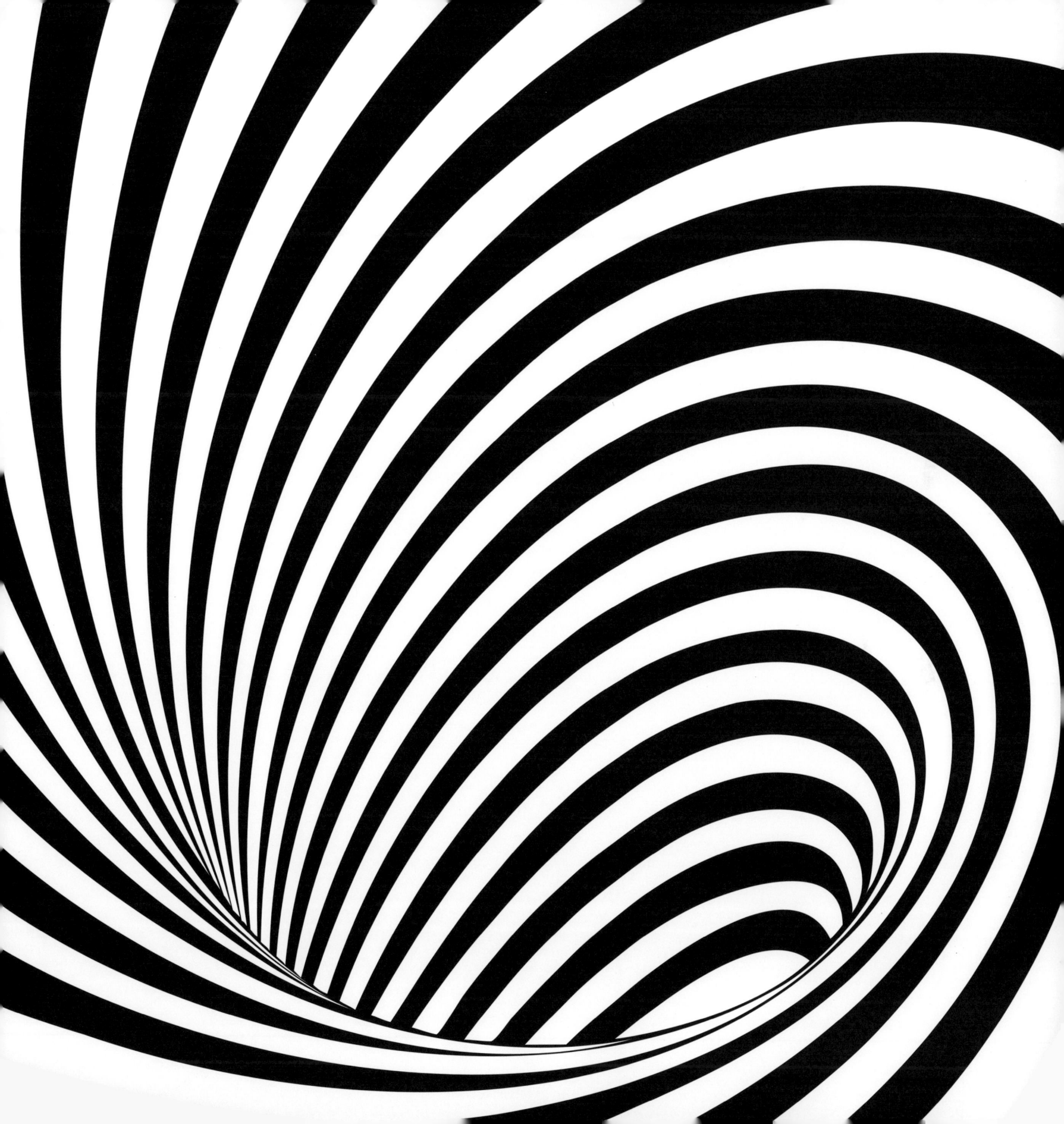

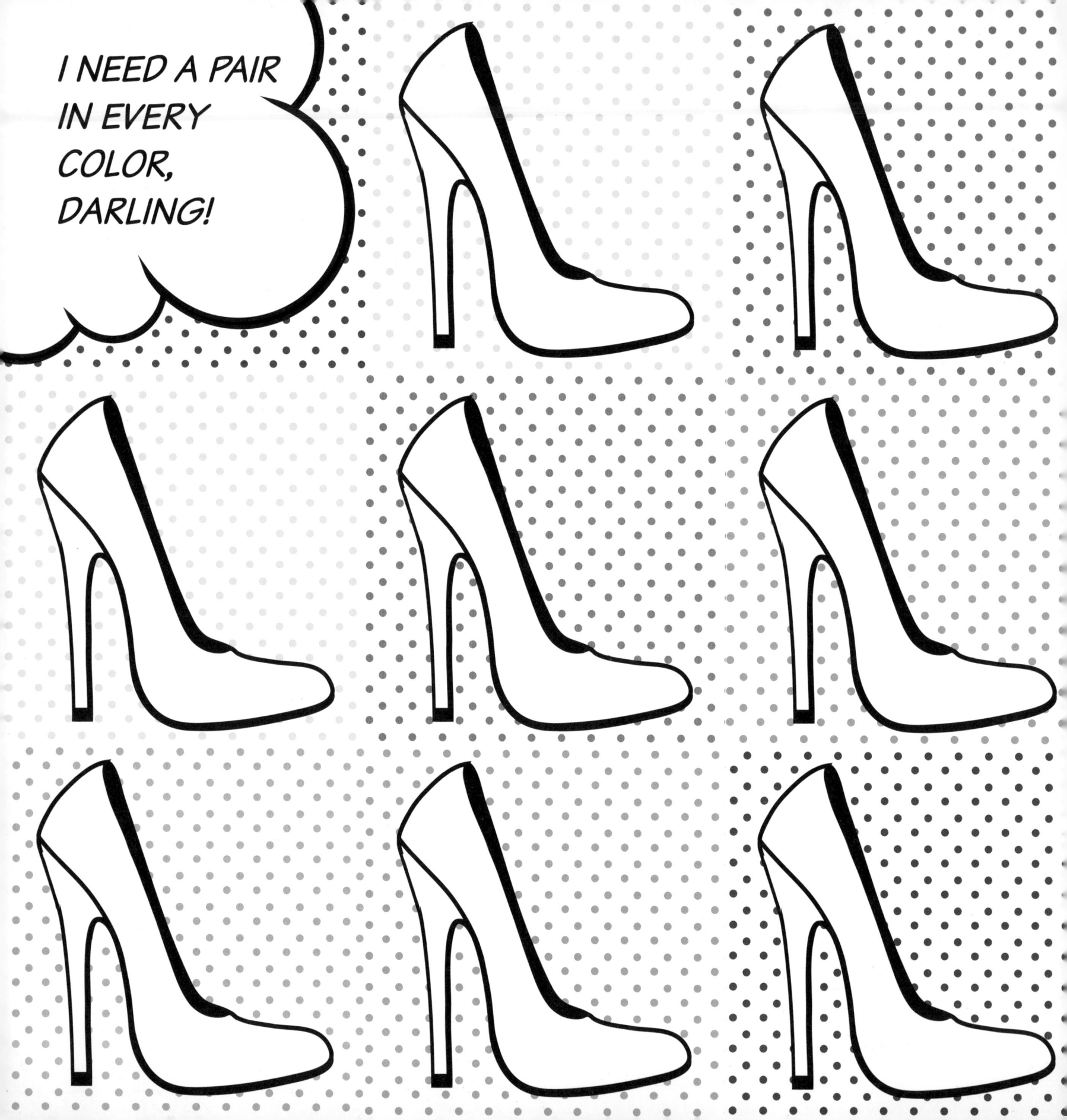
I NEED A PAIR IN EVERY COLOR, DARLING!

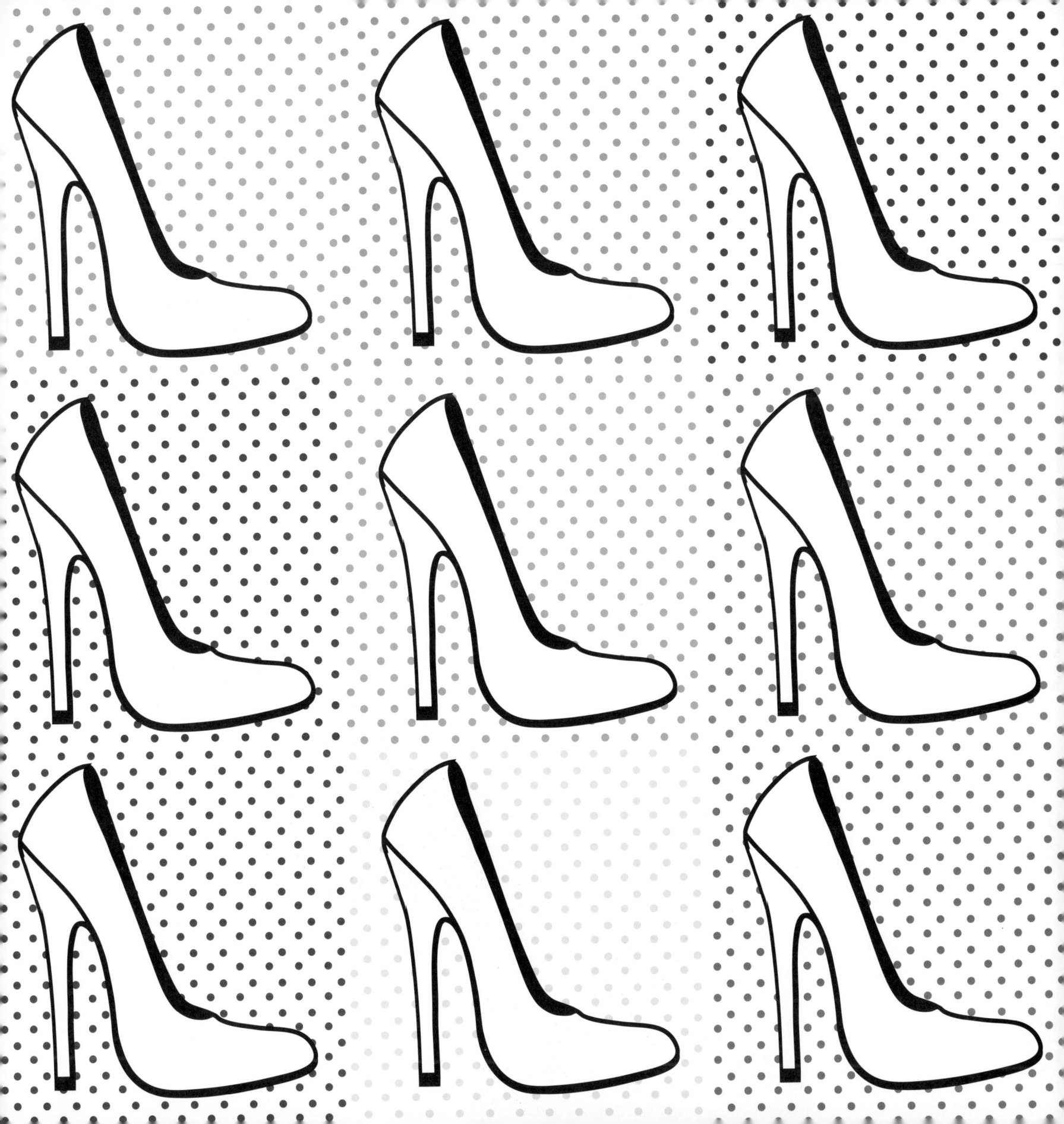

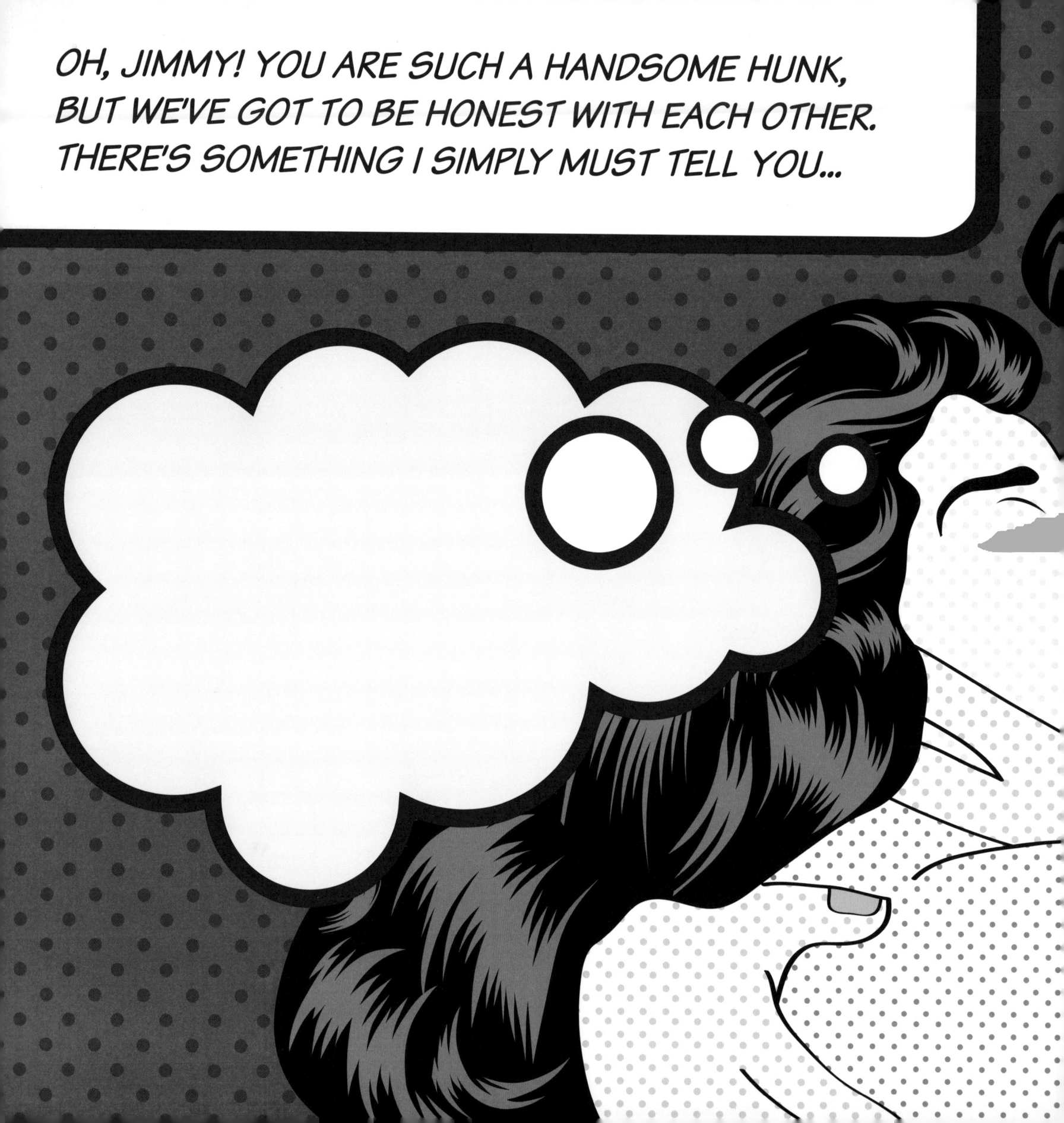
OH, JIMMY! YOU ARE SUCH A HANDSOME HUNK, BUT WE'VE GOT TO BE HONEST WITH EACH OTHER. THERE'S SOMETHING I SIMPLY MUST TELL YOU...

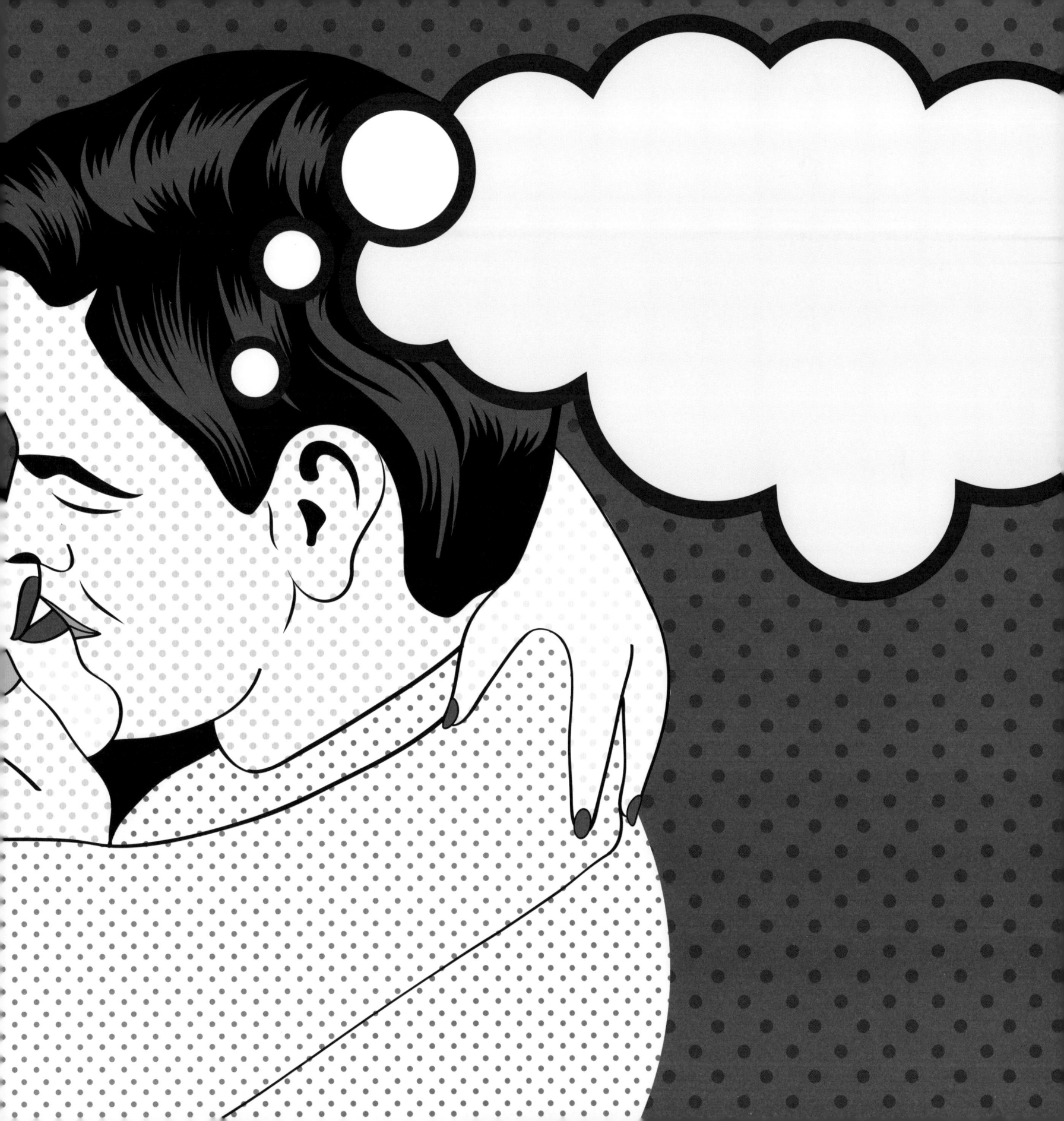

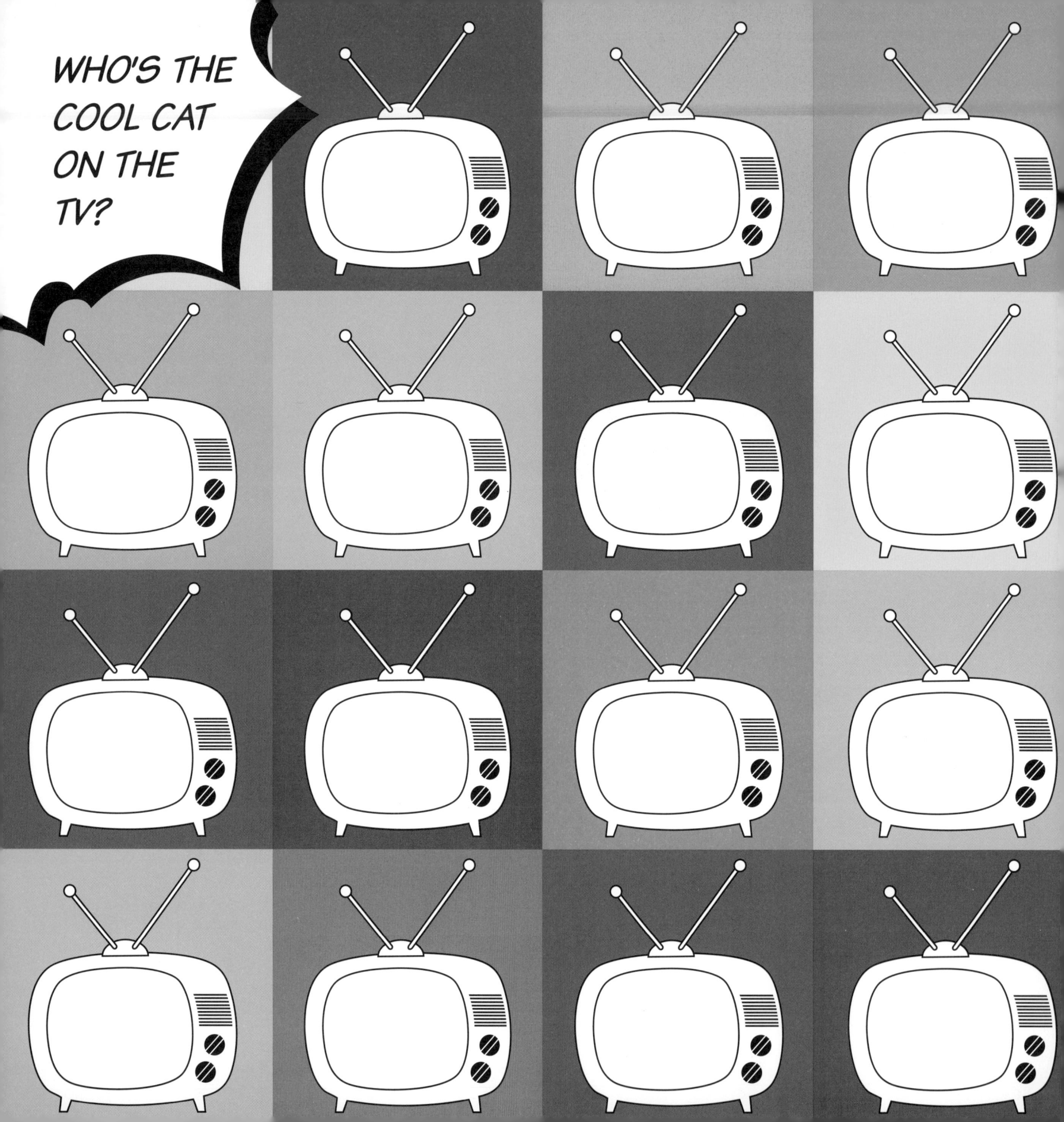
WHO'S THE COOL CAT ON THE TV?

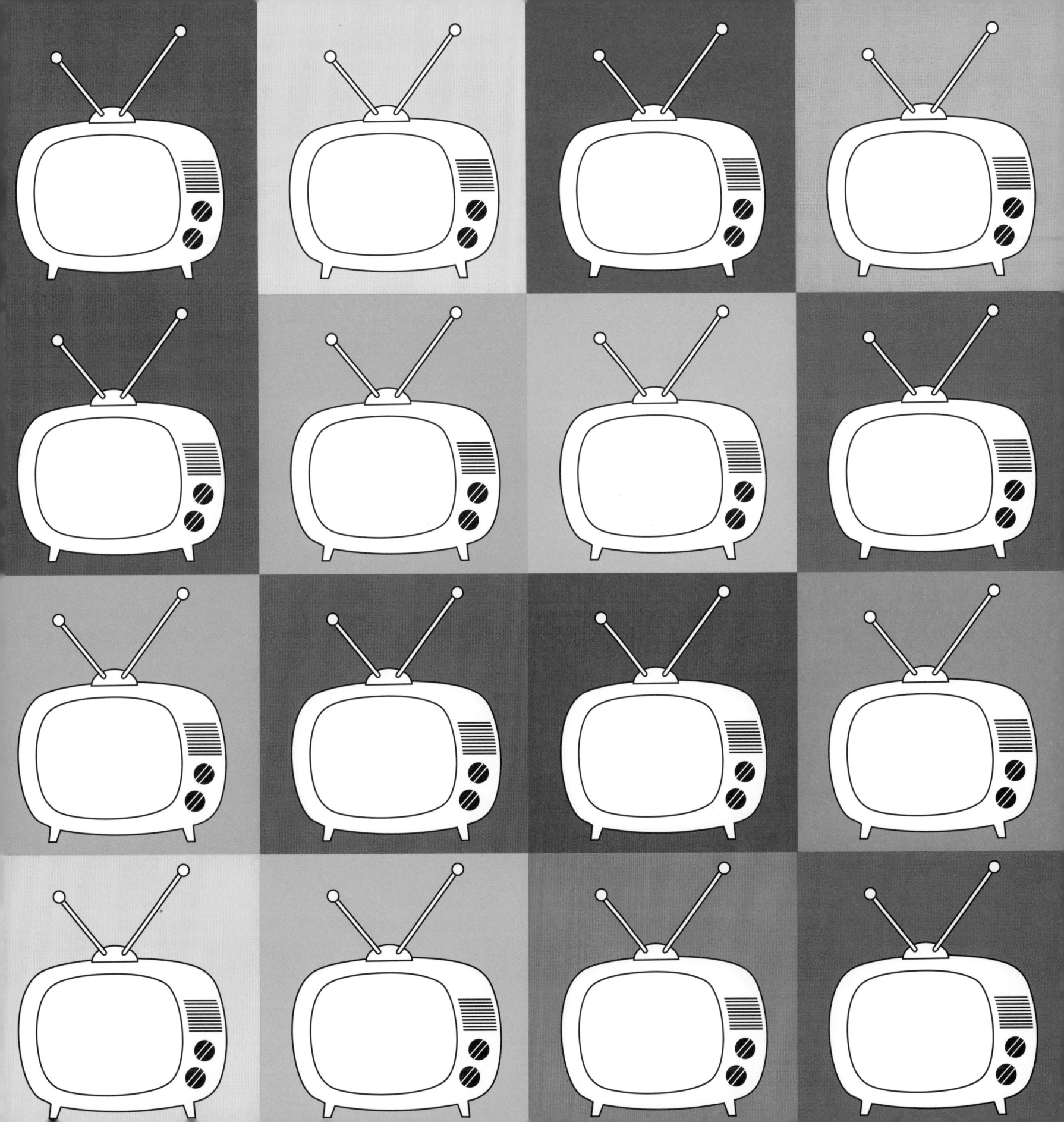

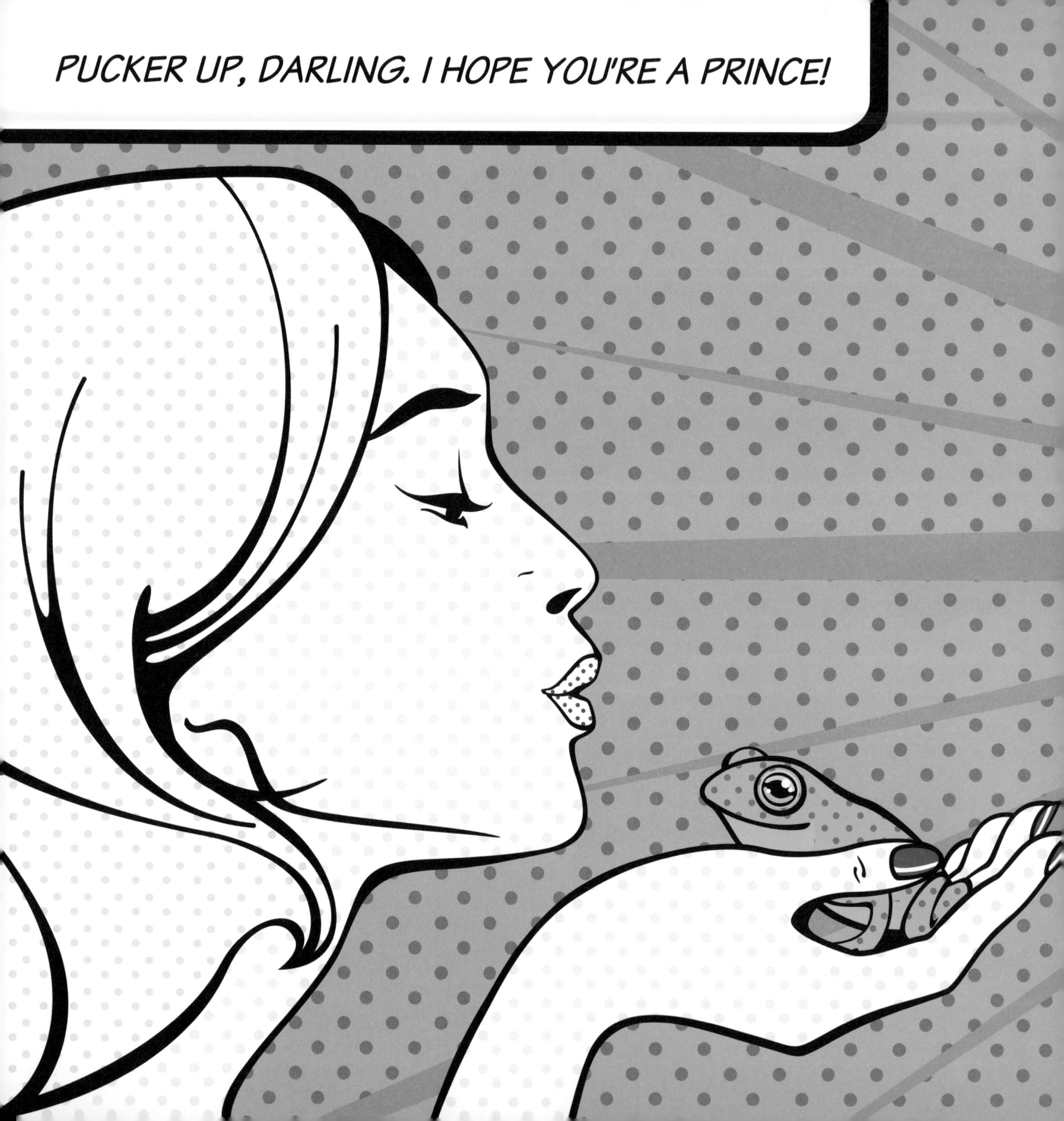
PUCKER UP, DARLING. I HOPE YOU'RE A PRINCE!

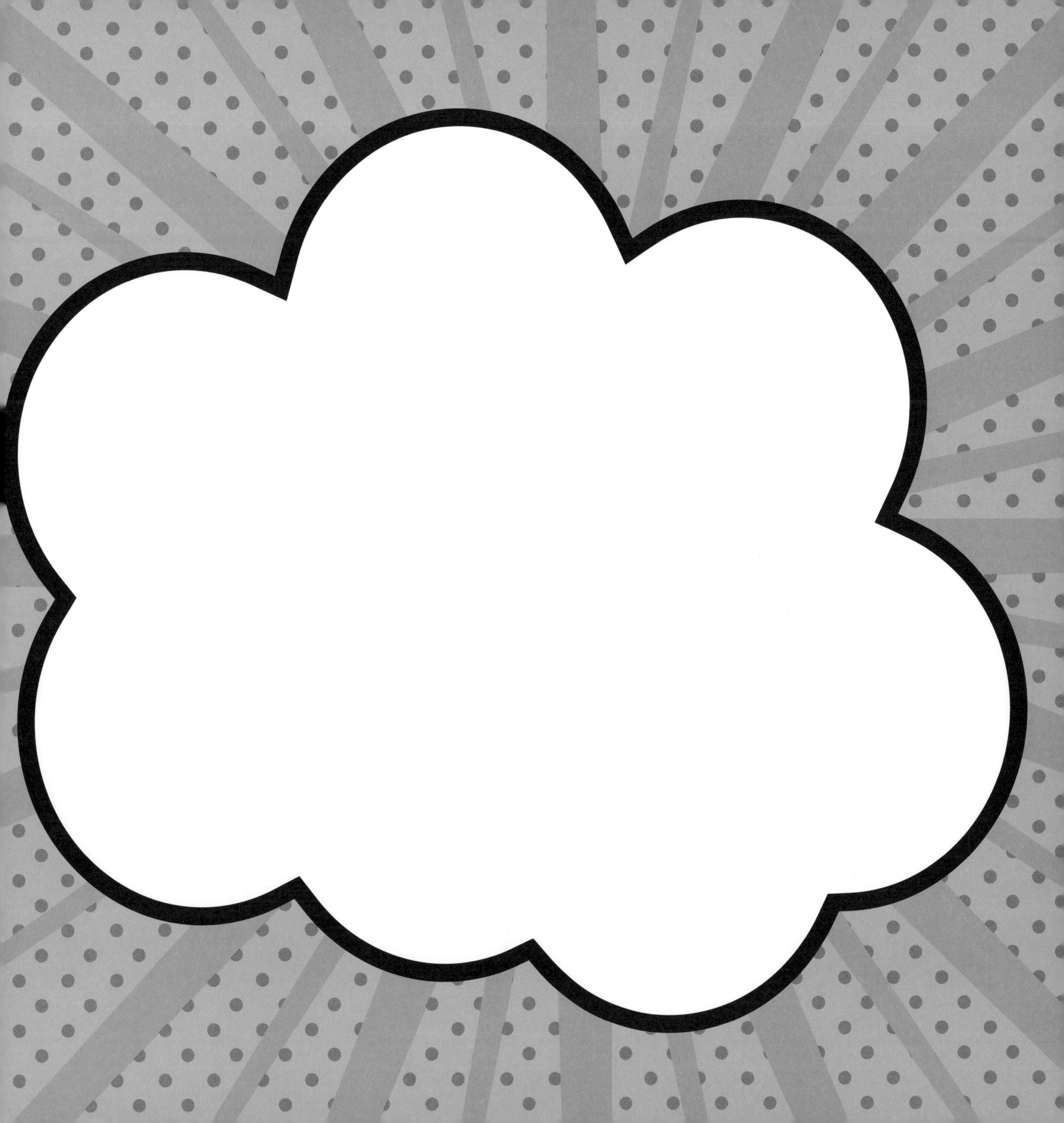

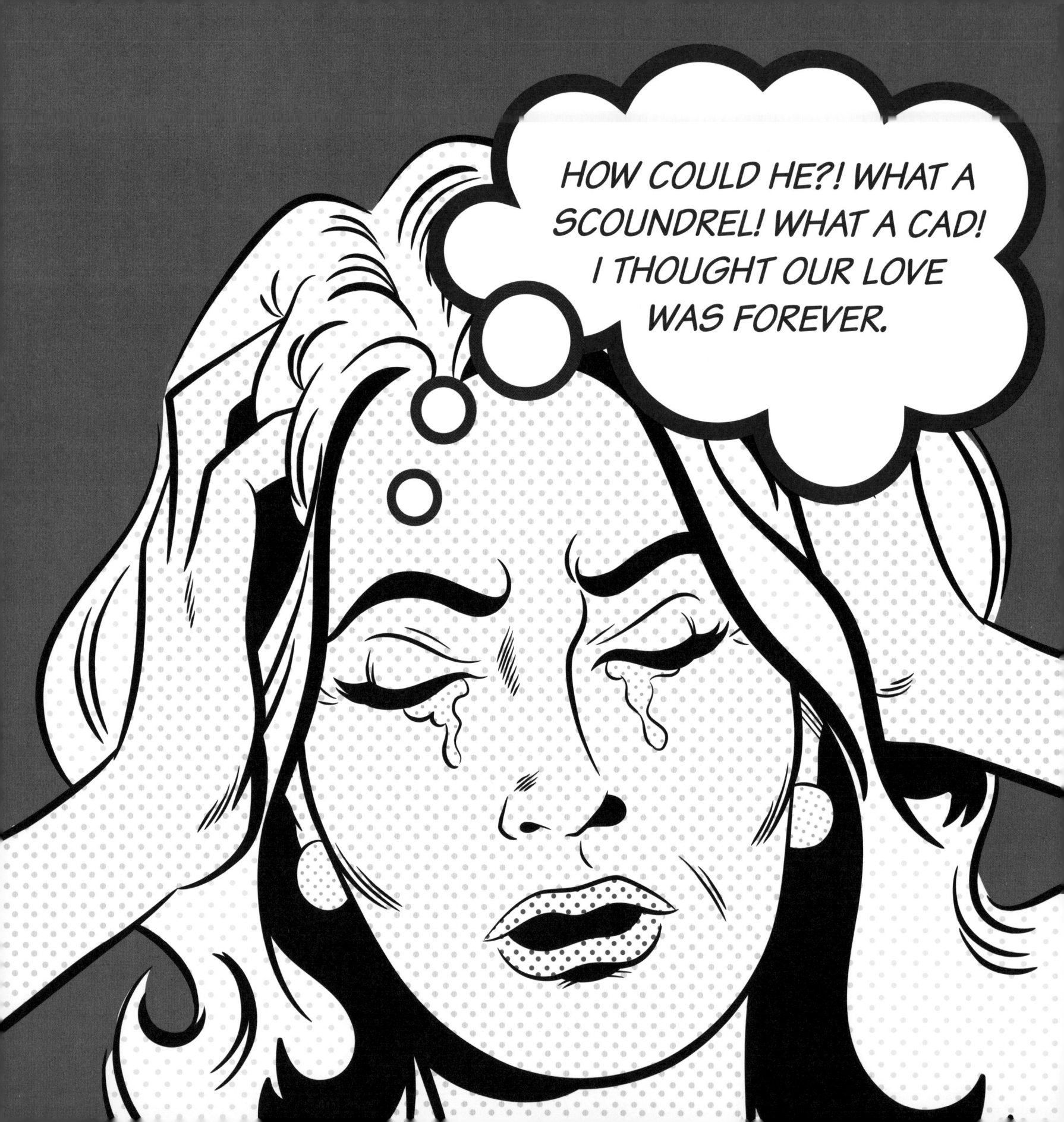
HOW COULD HE?! WHAT A SCOUNDREL! WHAT A CAD! I THOUGHT OUR LOVE WAS FOREVER.

COMPLETE THIS RETRO HONEY'S PERFECTLY HIP THREADS.

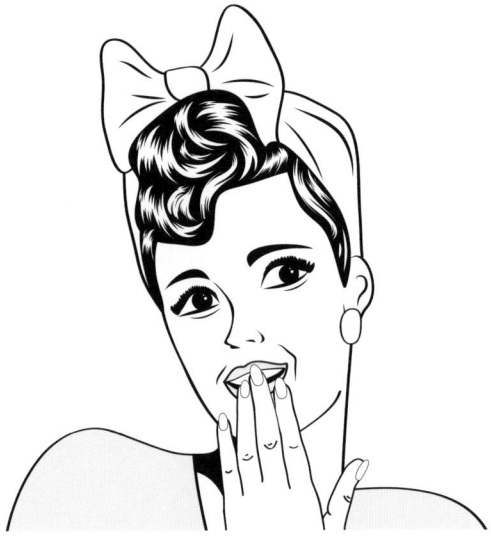

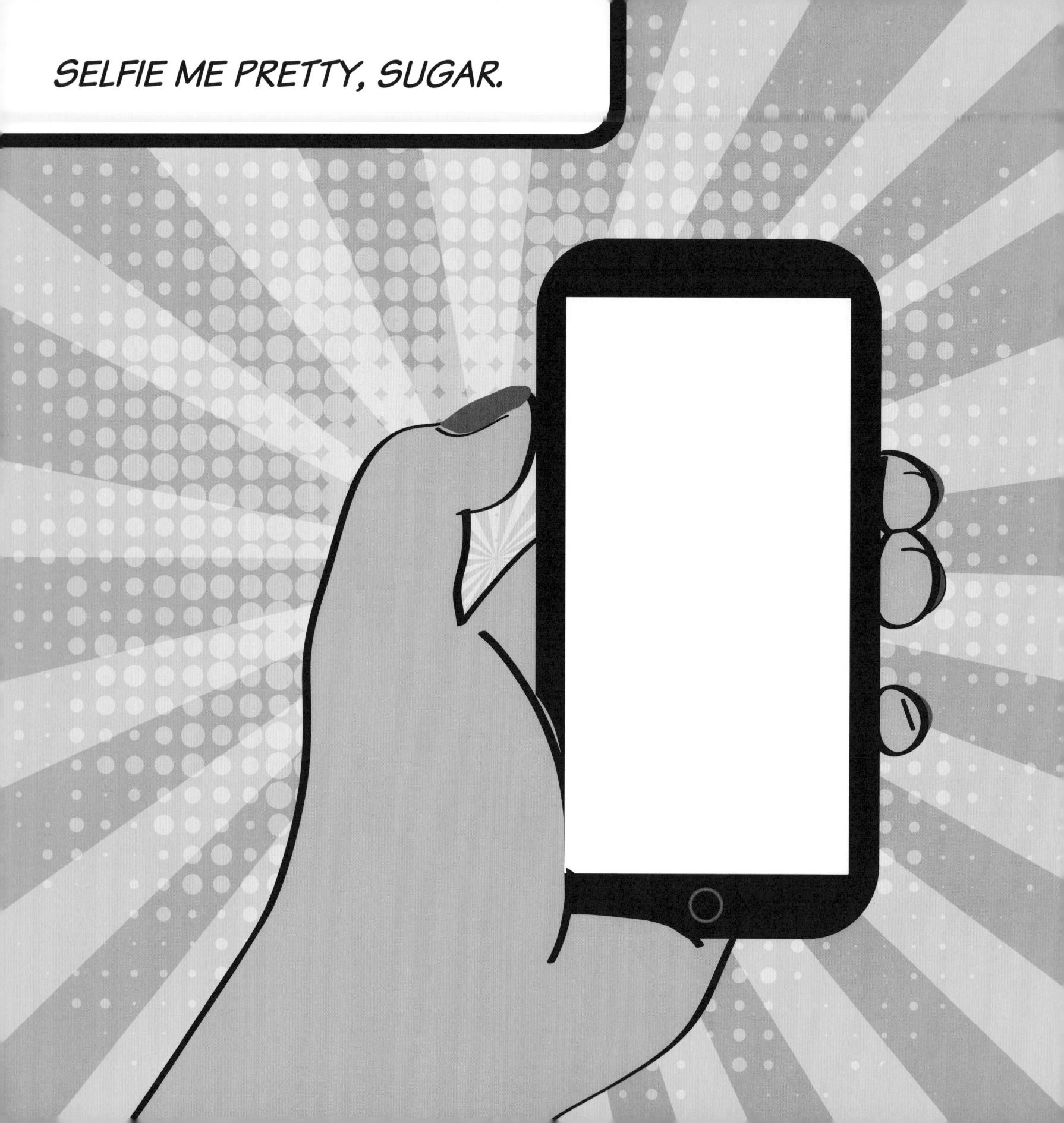
SELFIE ME PRETTY, SUGAR.

STYLE THE DOLL FOR THESE LIPS.

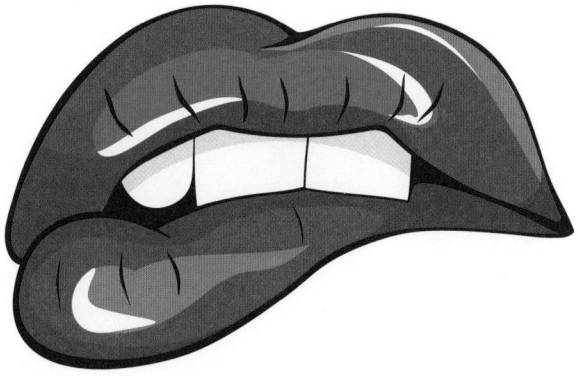

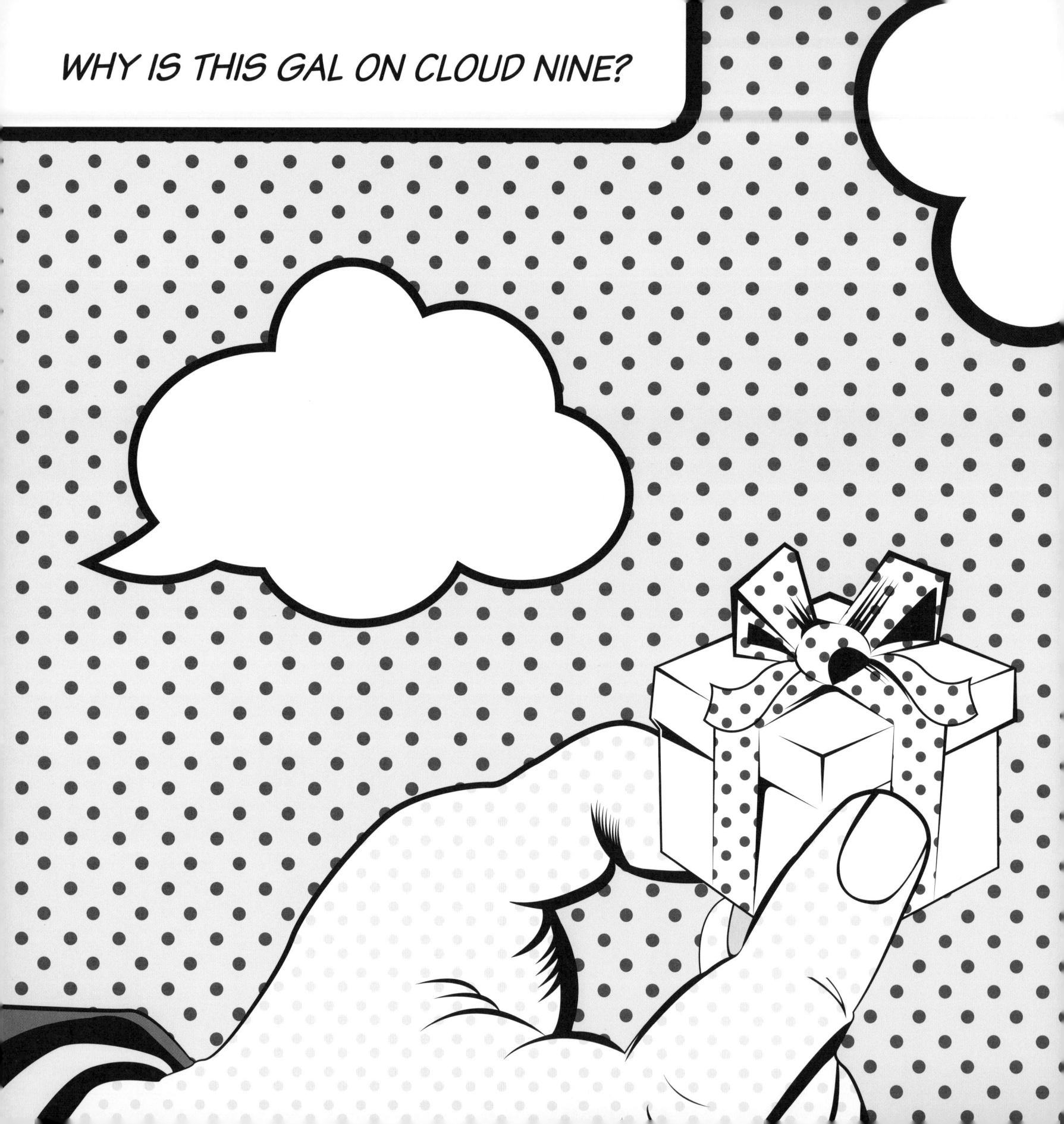
WHY IS THIS GAL ON CLOUD NINE?

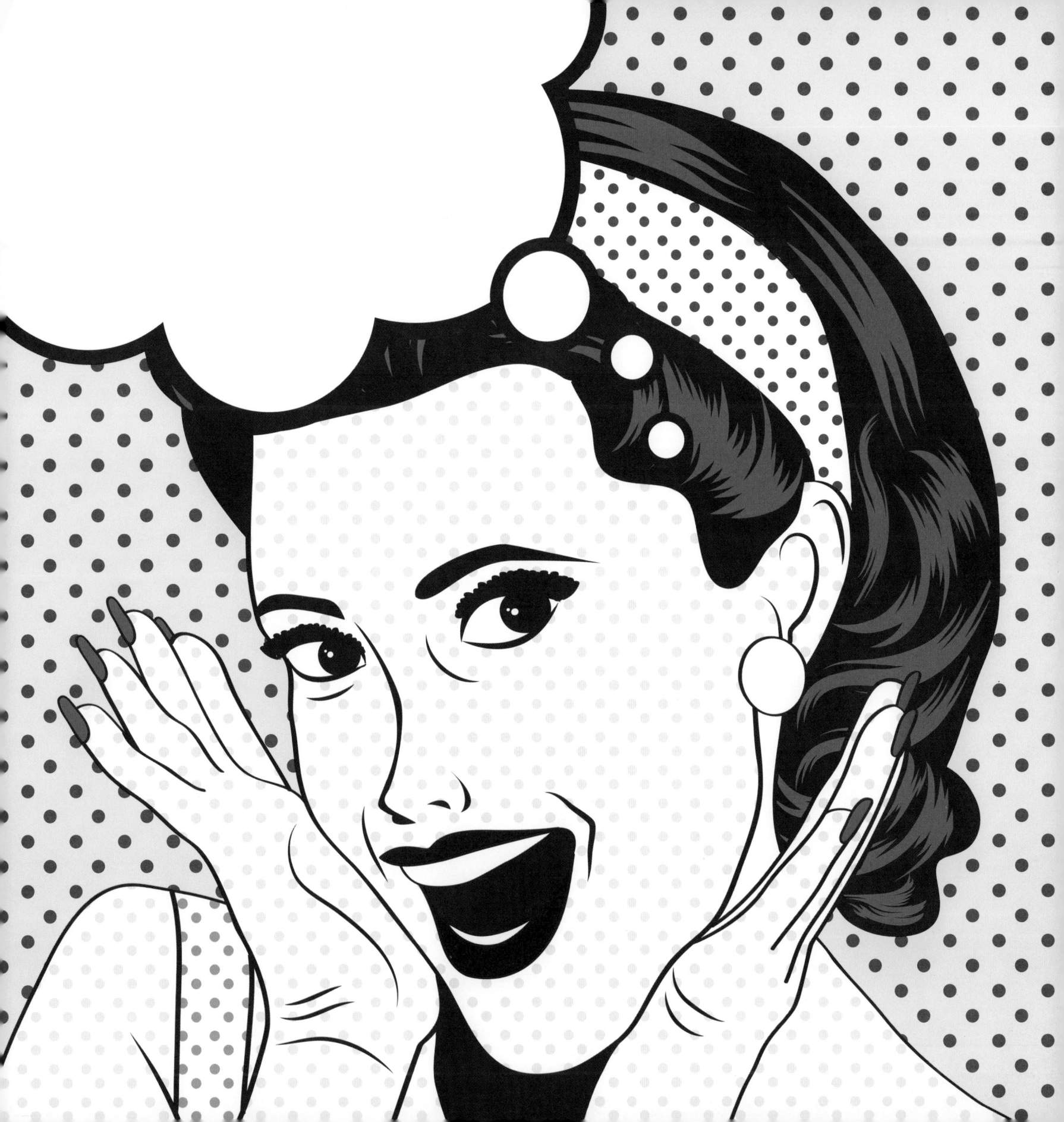

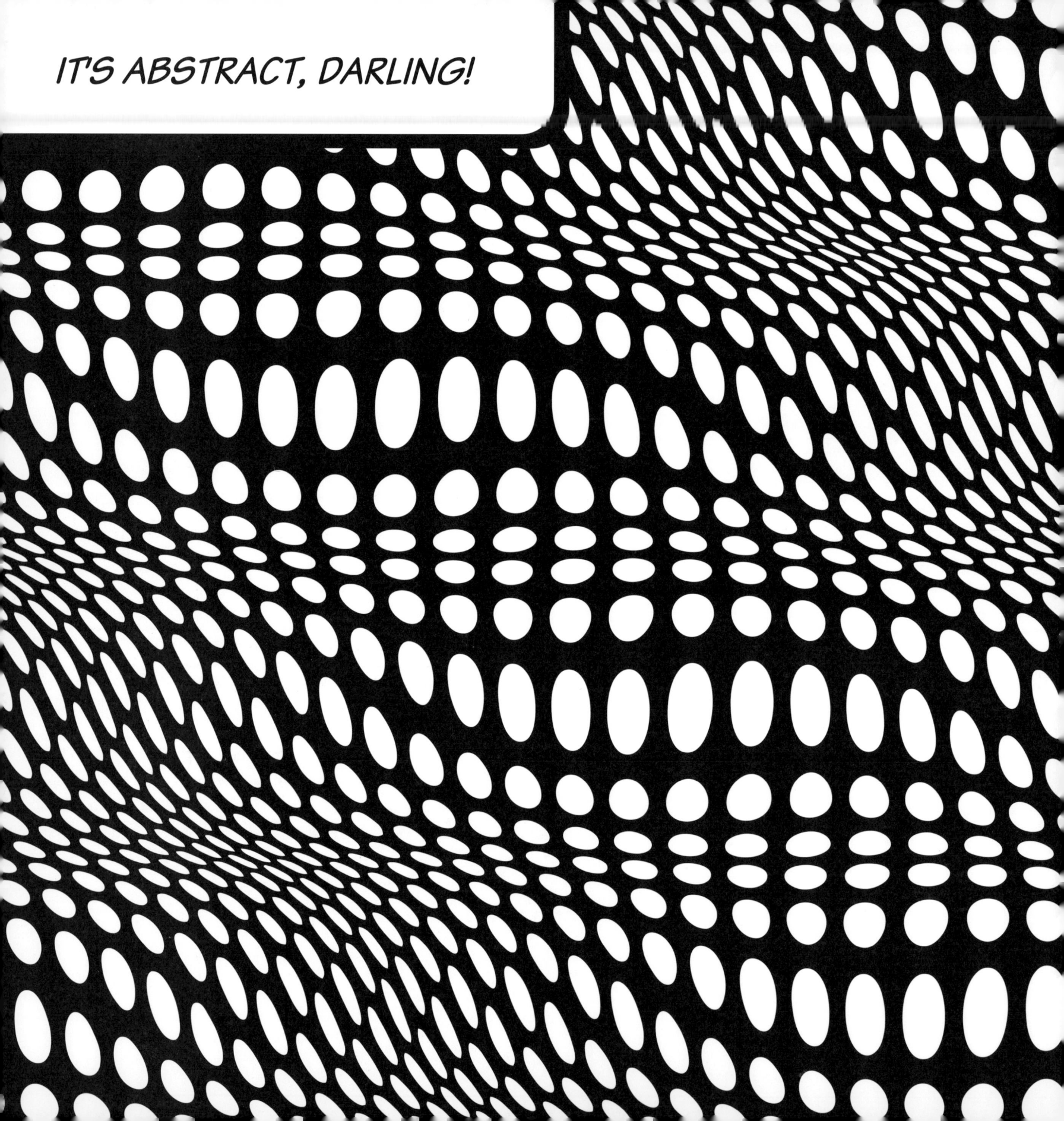
IT'S ABSTRACT, DARLING!

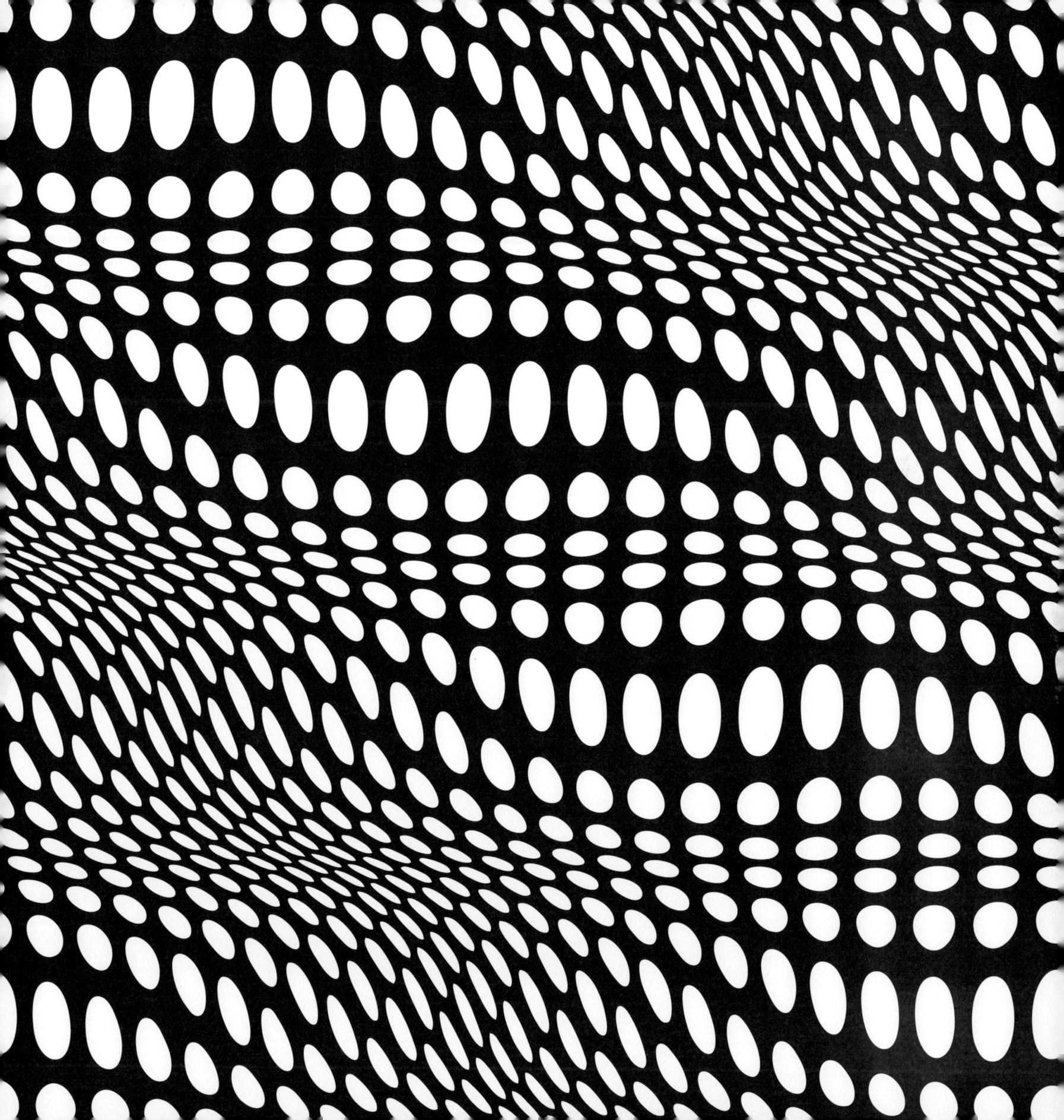

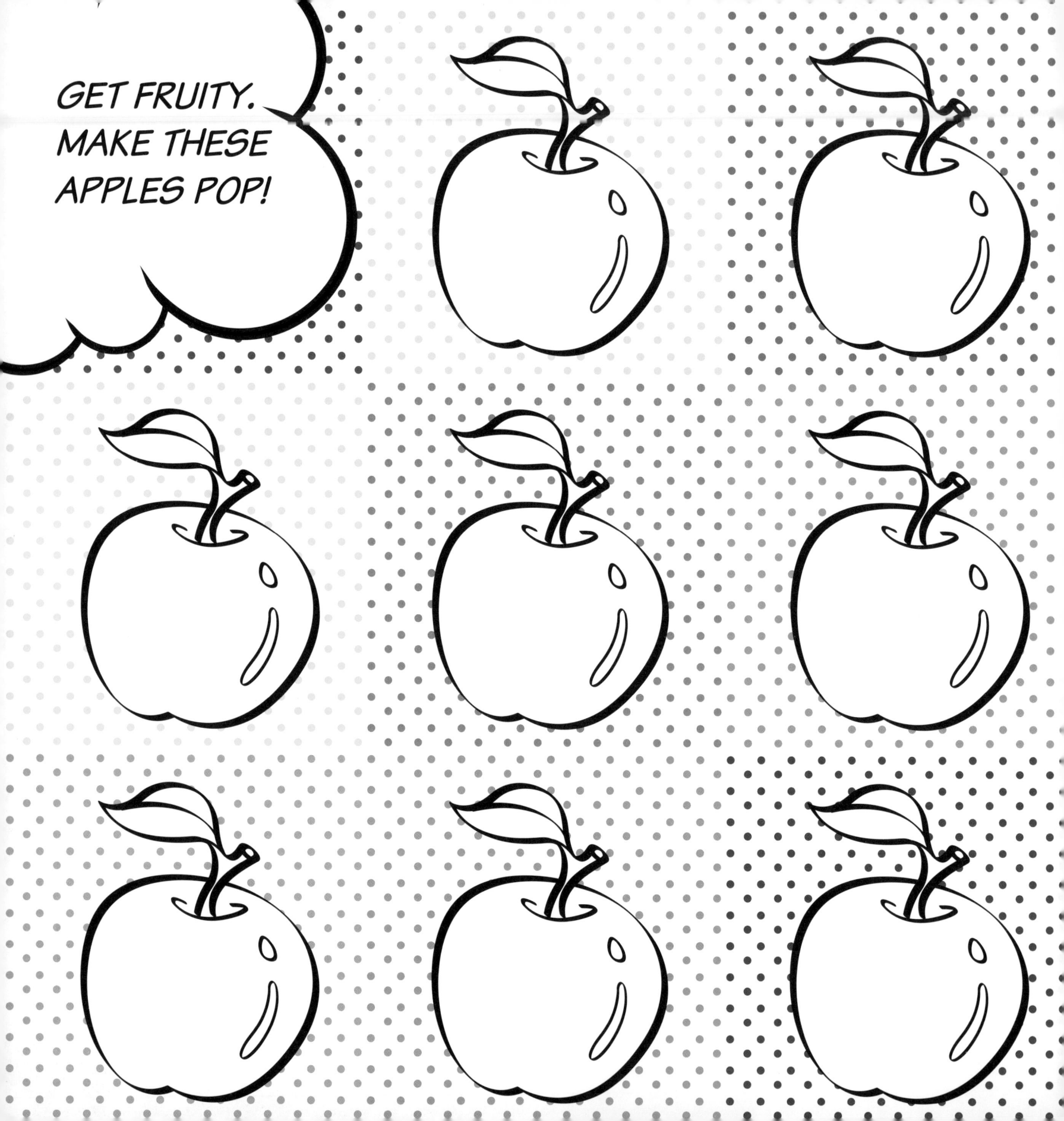
GET FRUITY.
MAKE THESE
APPLES POP!

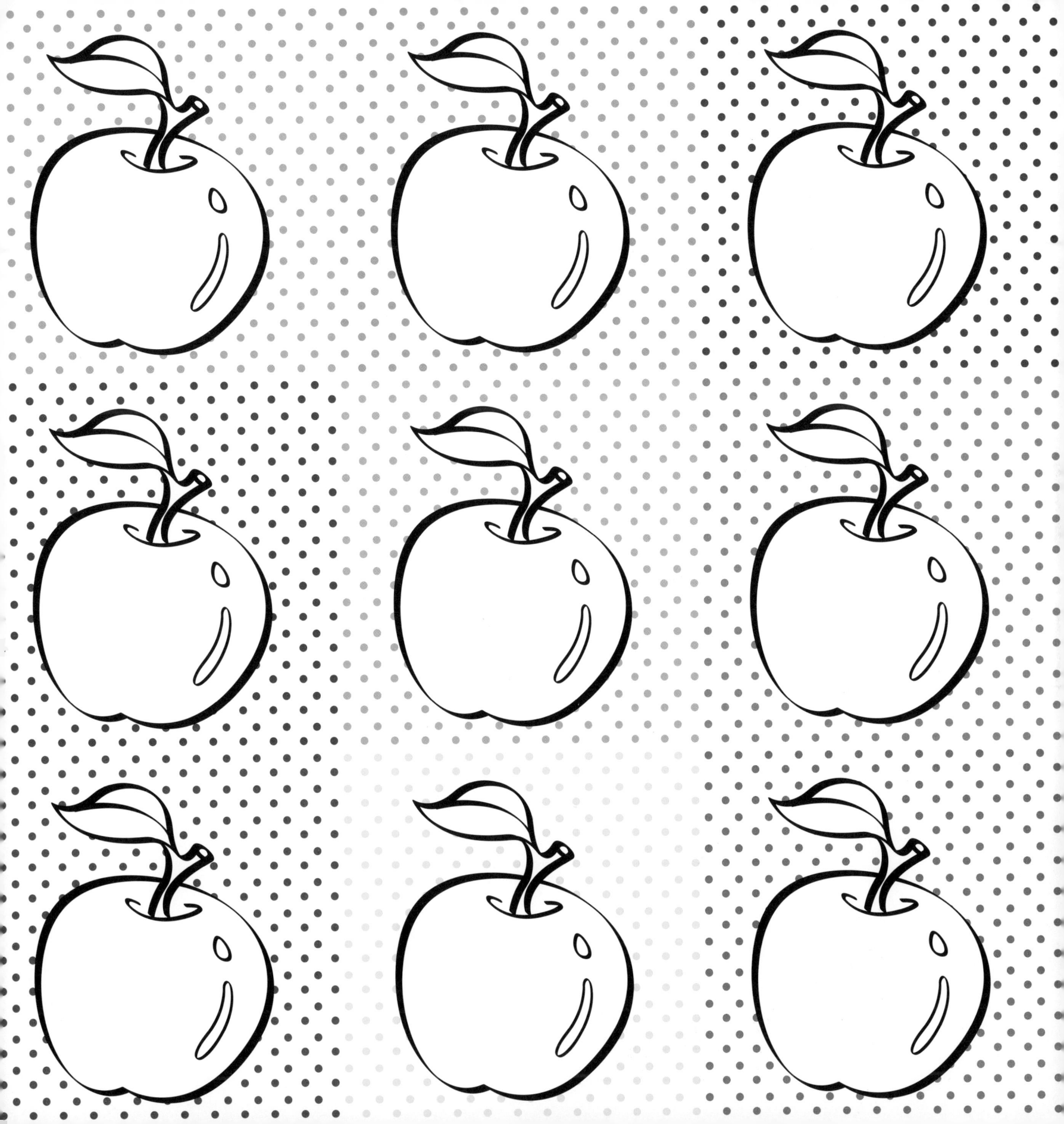

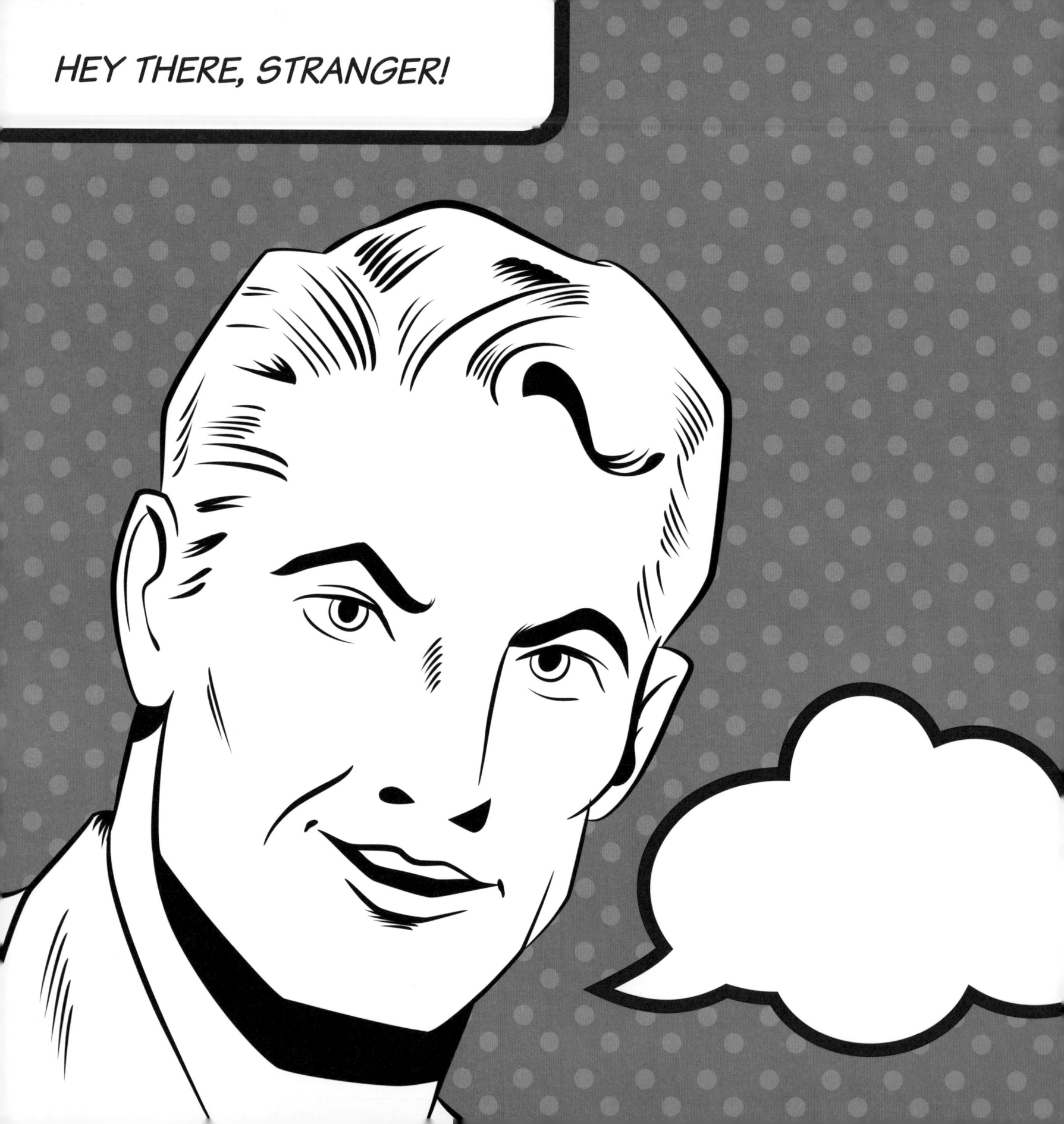
HEY THERE, STRANGER!

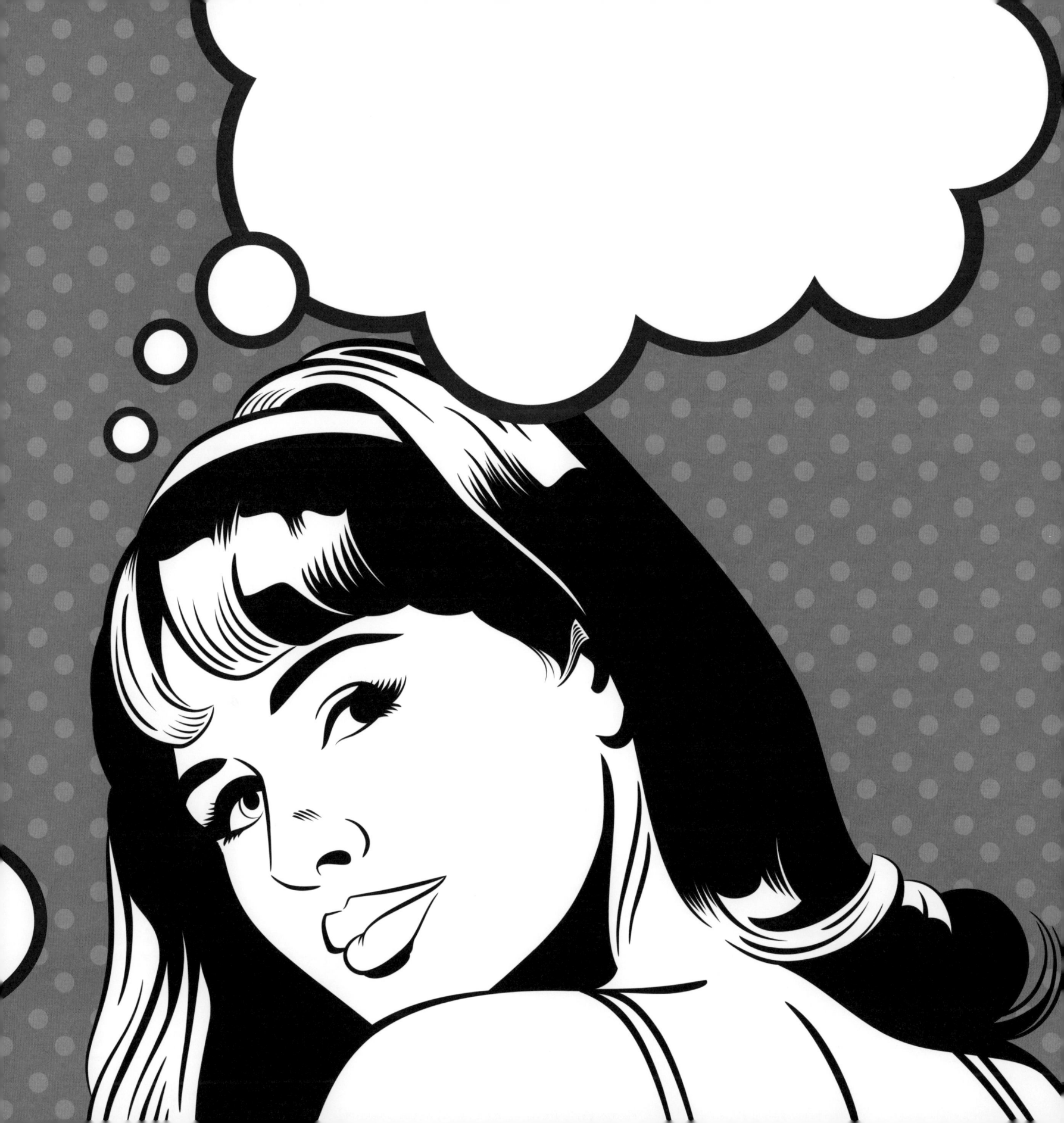

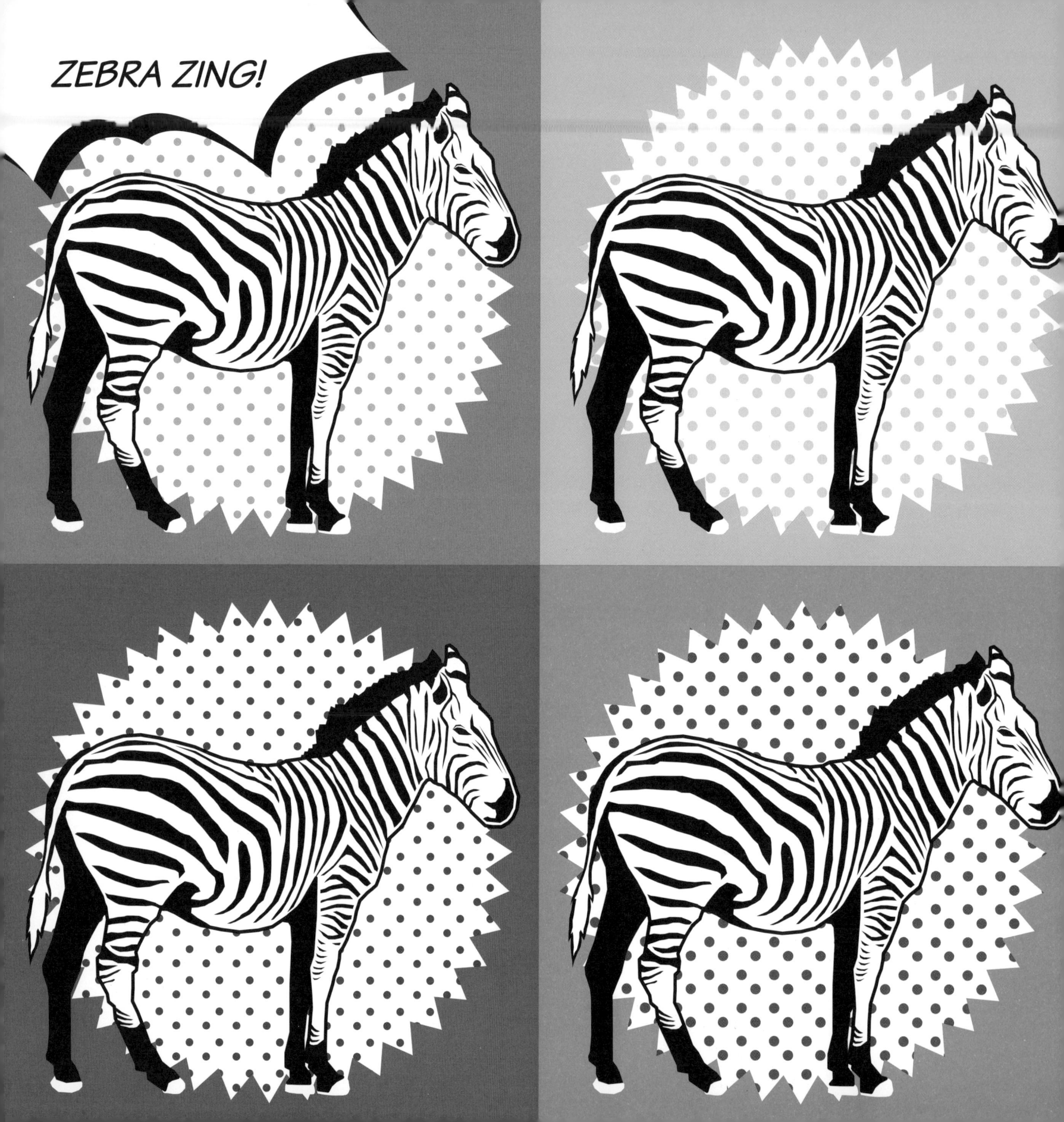
ZEBRA ZING!

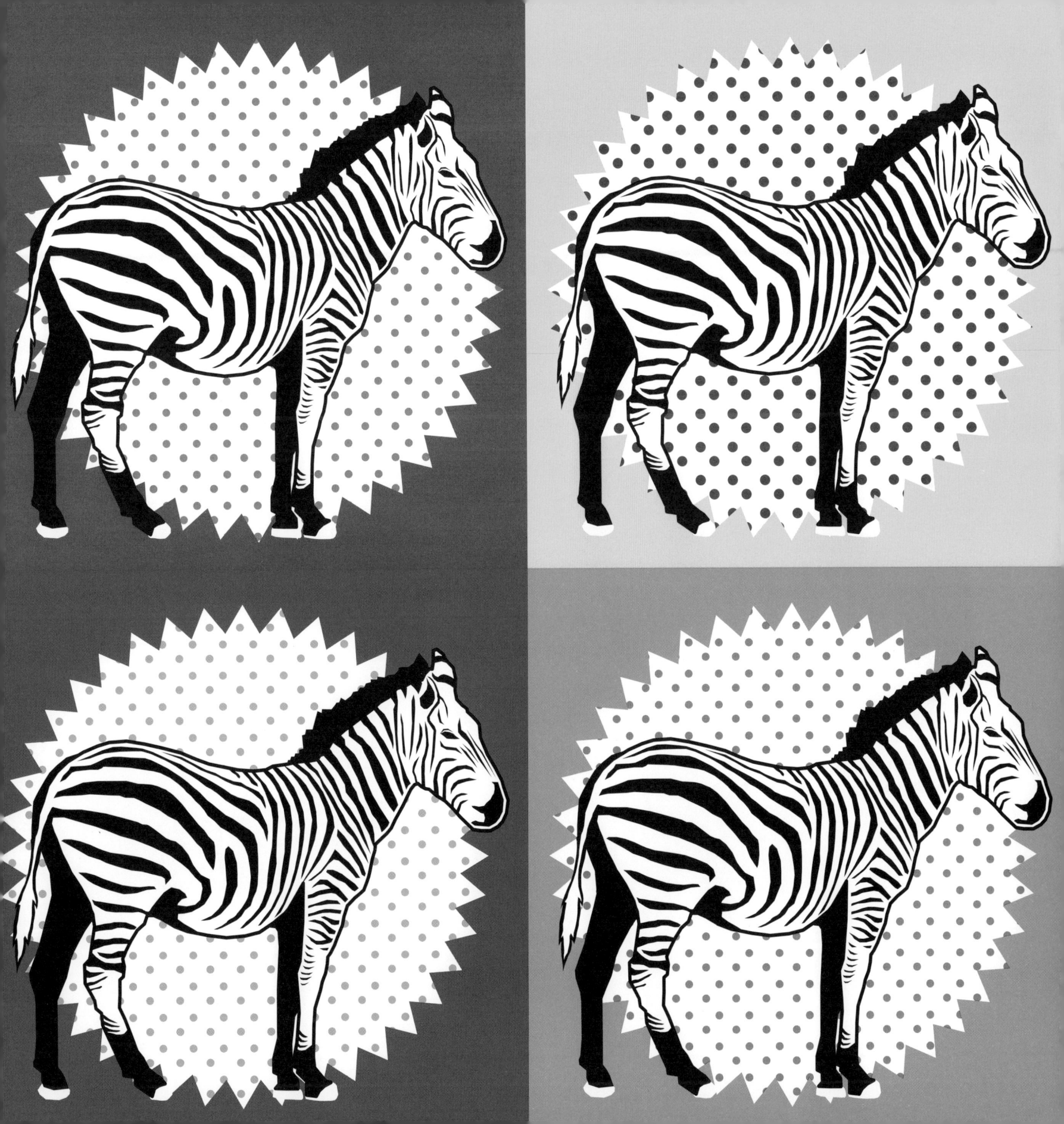

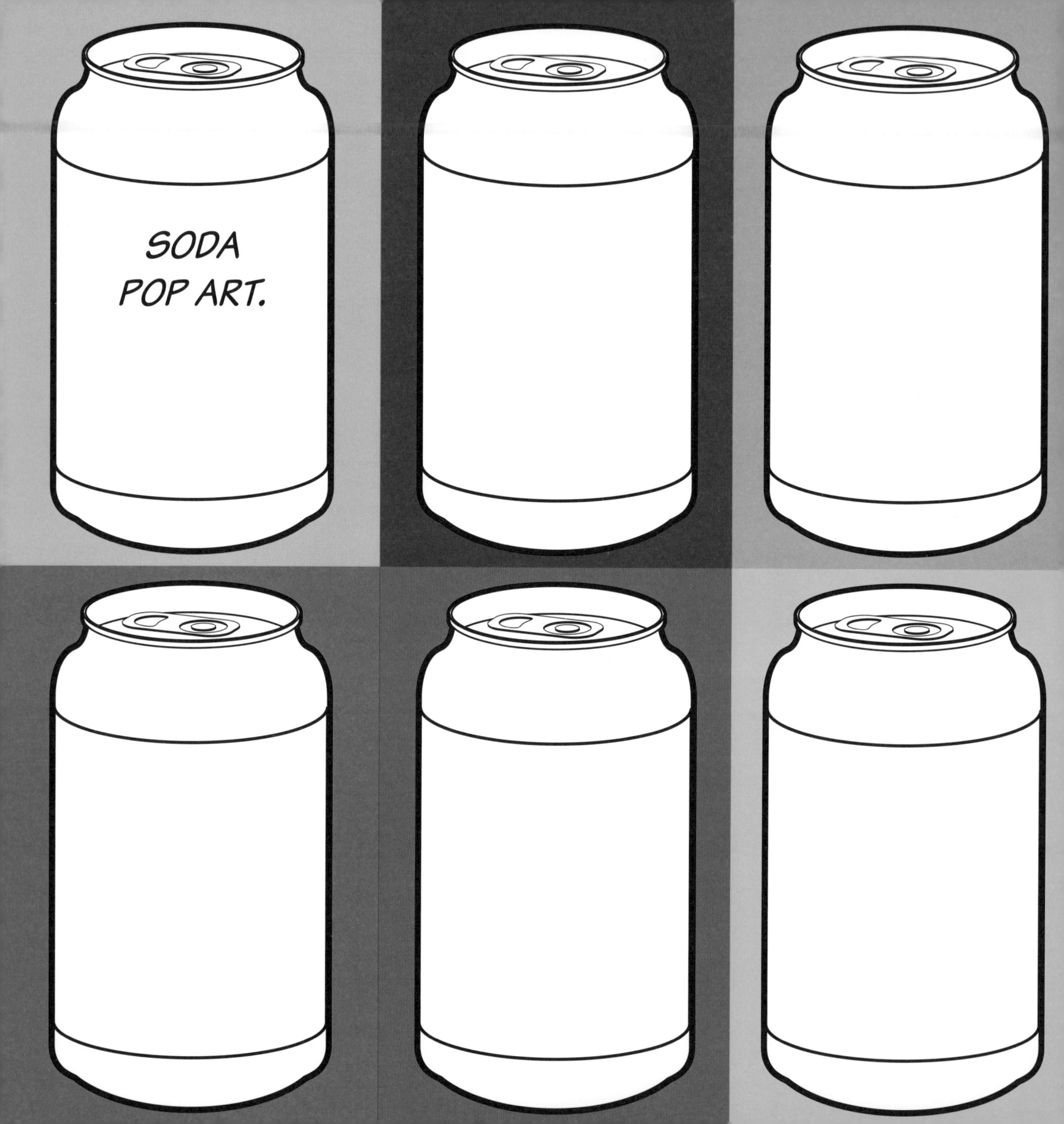
SODA
POP ART.

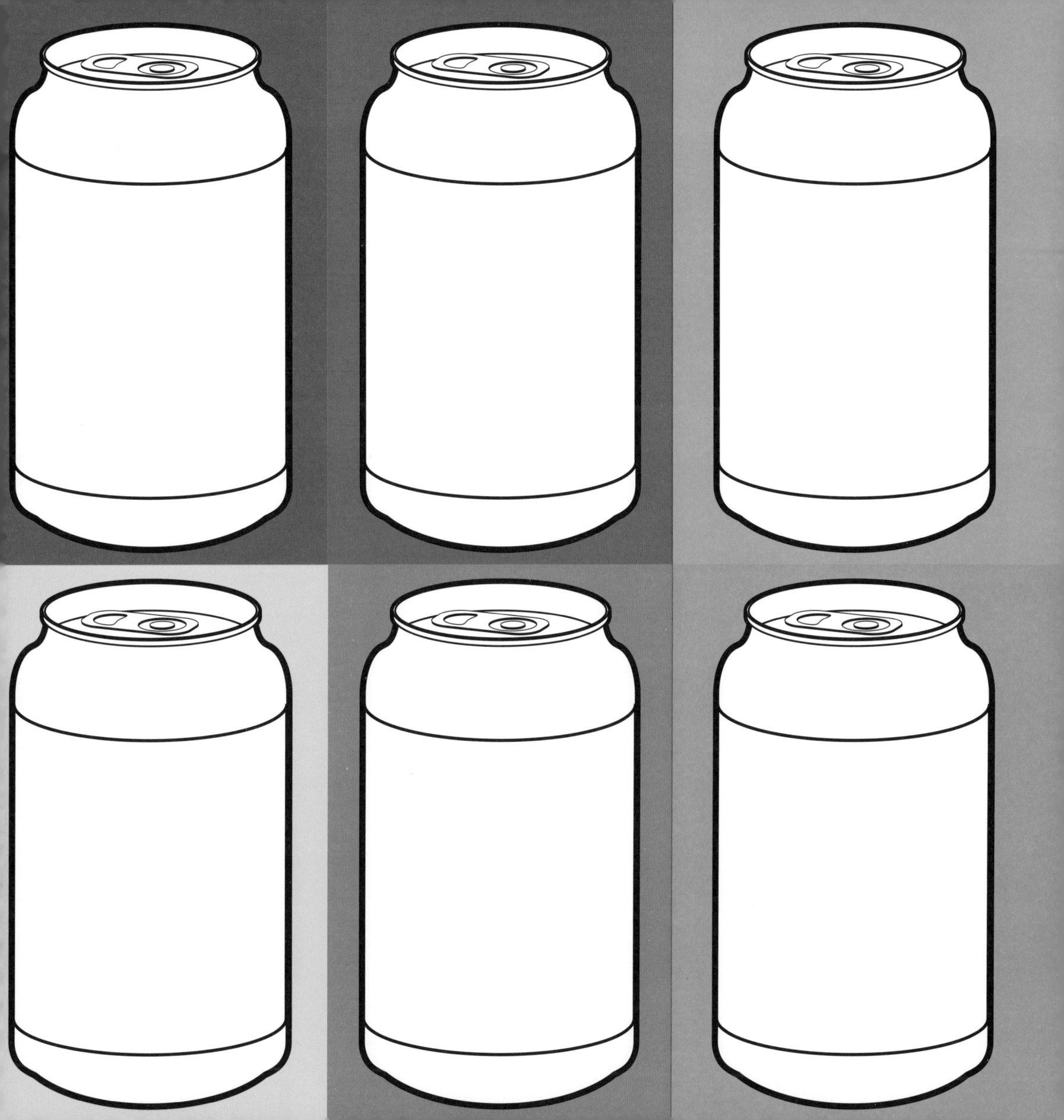

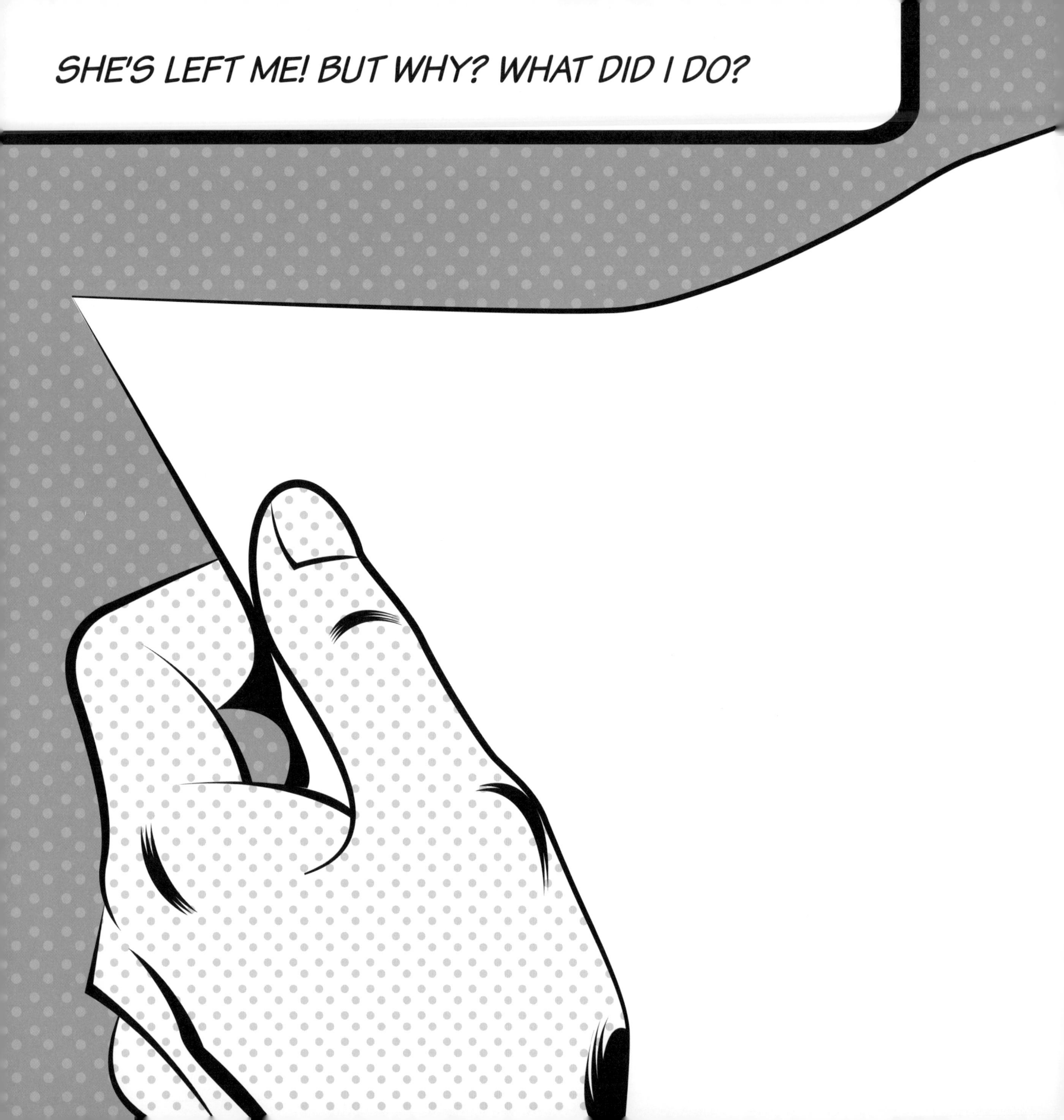
SHE'S LEFT ME! BUT WHY? WHAT DID I DO?

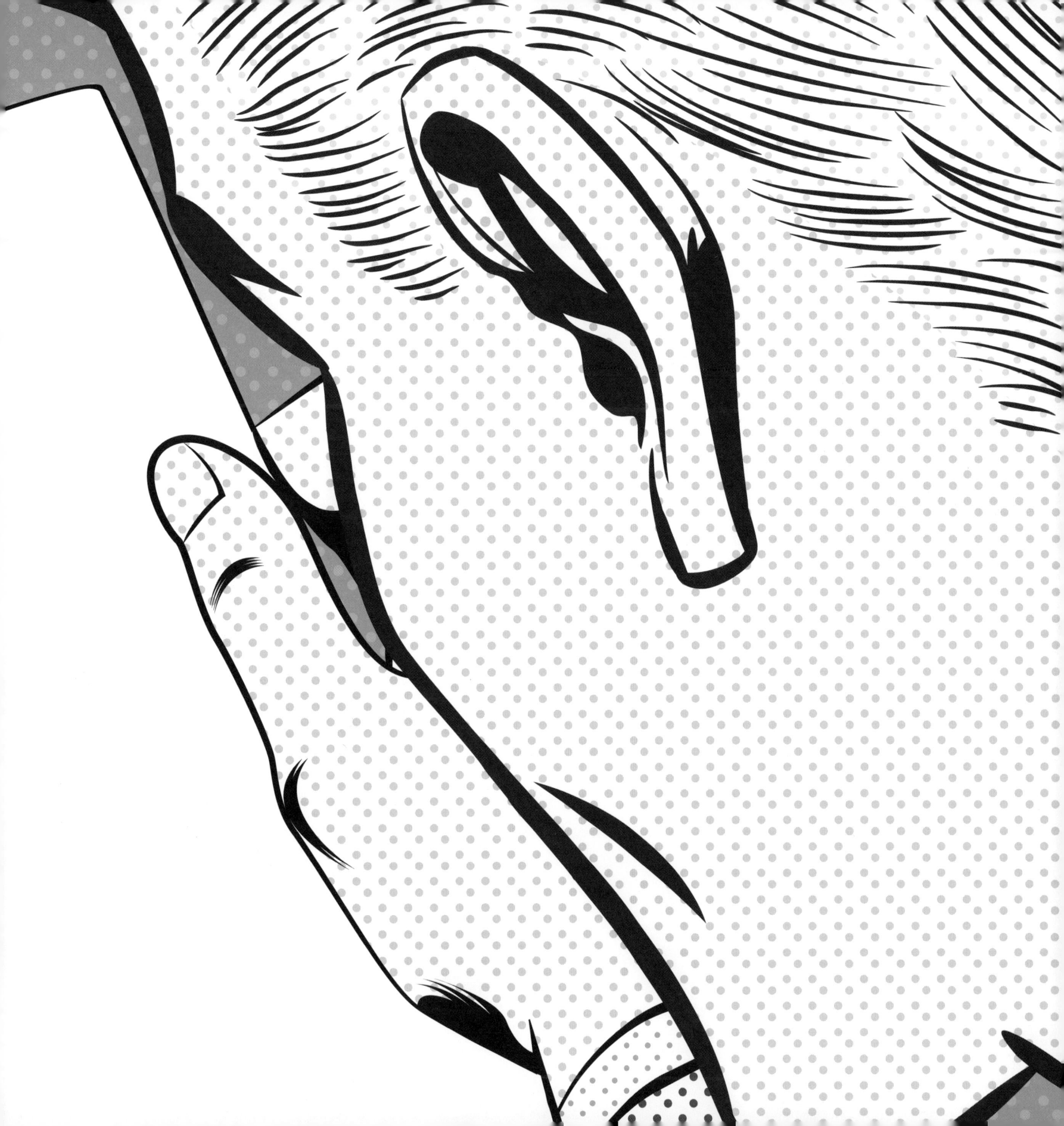

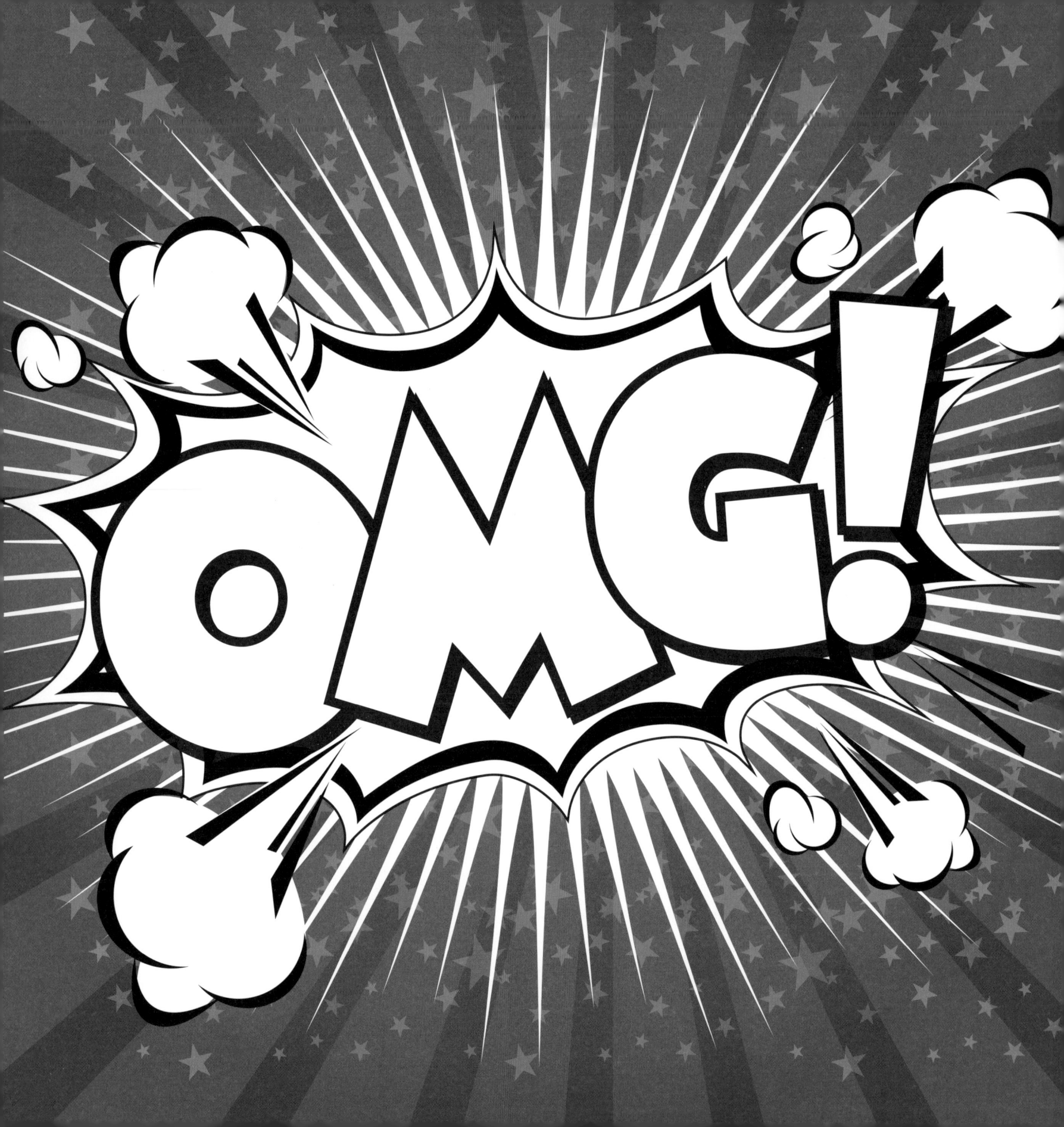
OMG!

PARTY!

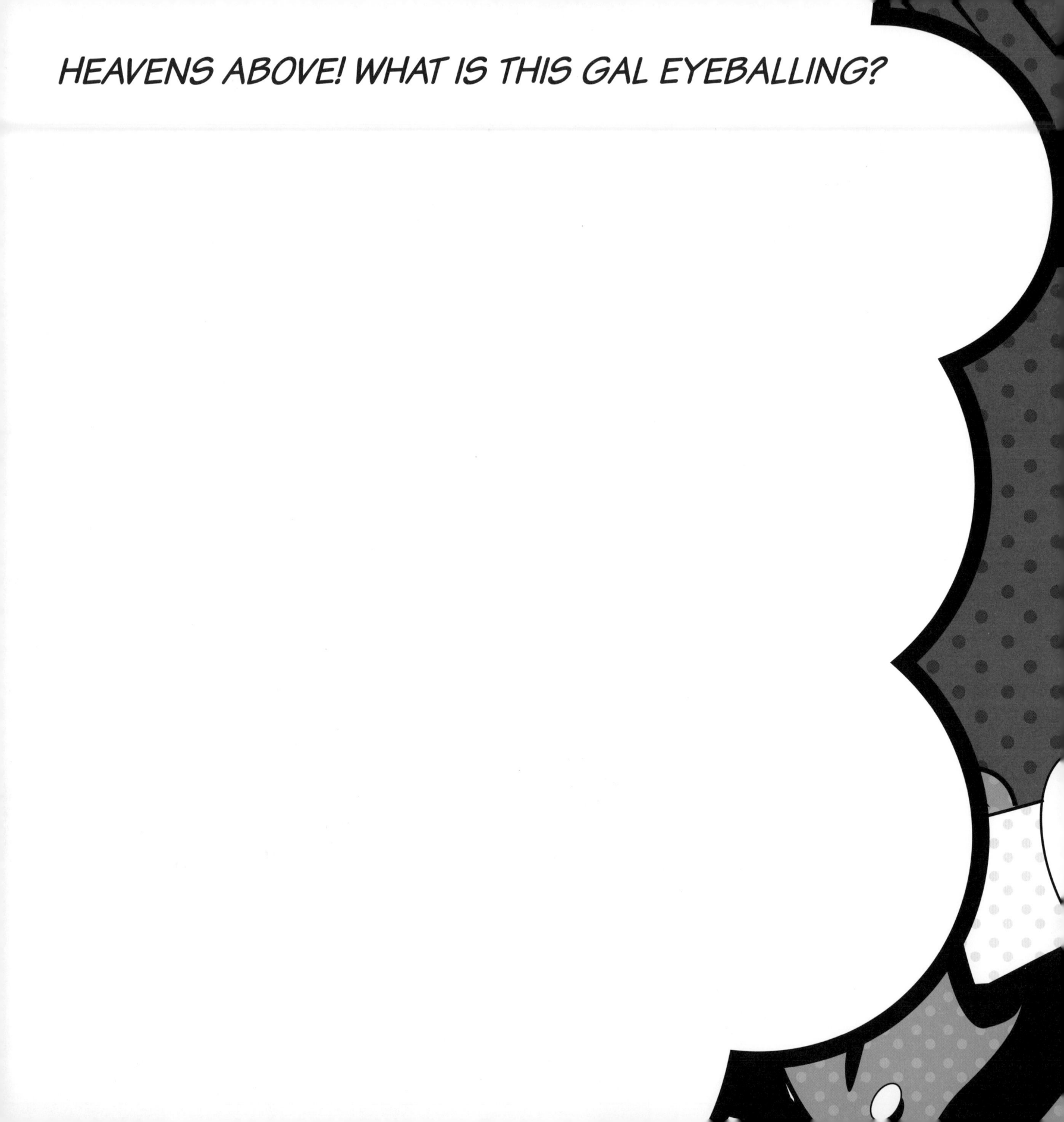
HEAVENS ABOVE! WHAT IS THIS GAL EYEBALLING?

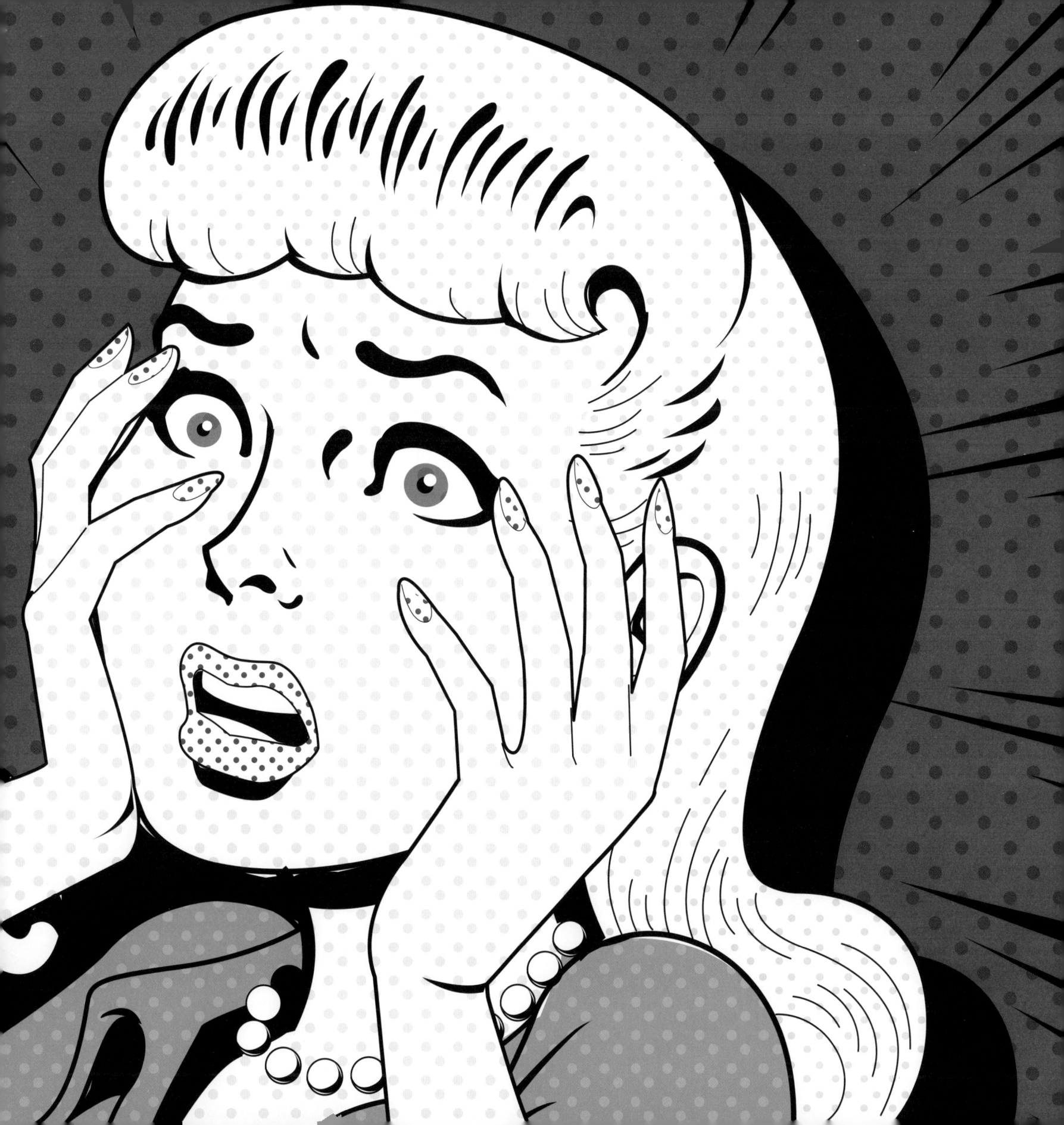

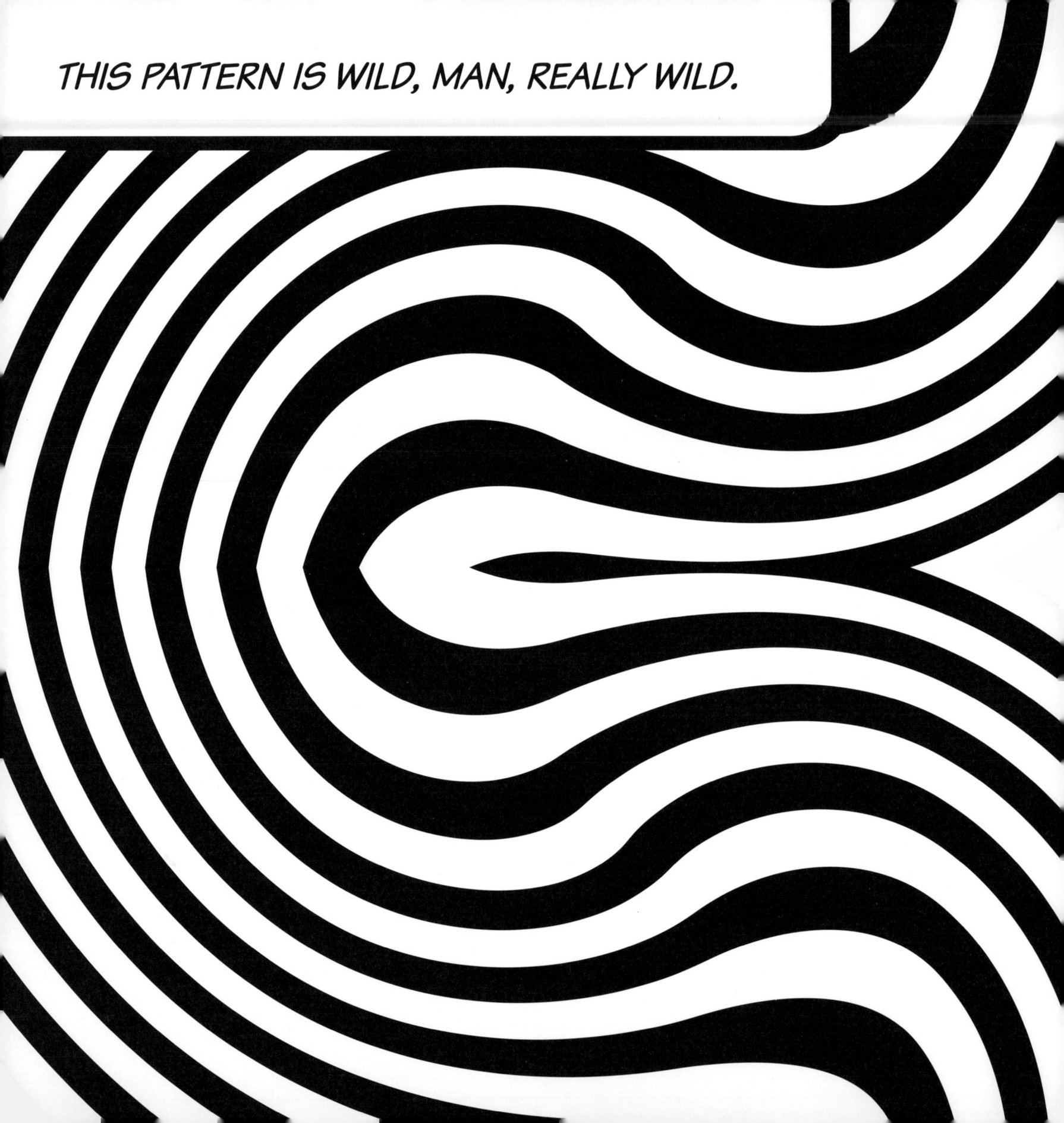
THIS PATTERN IS WILD, MAN, REALLY WILD.

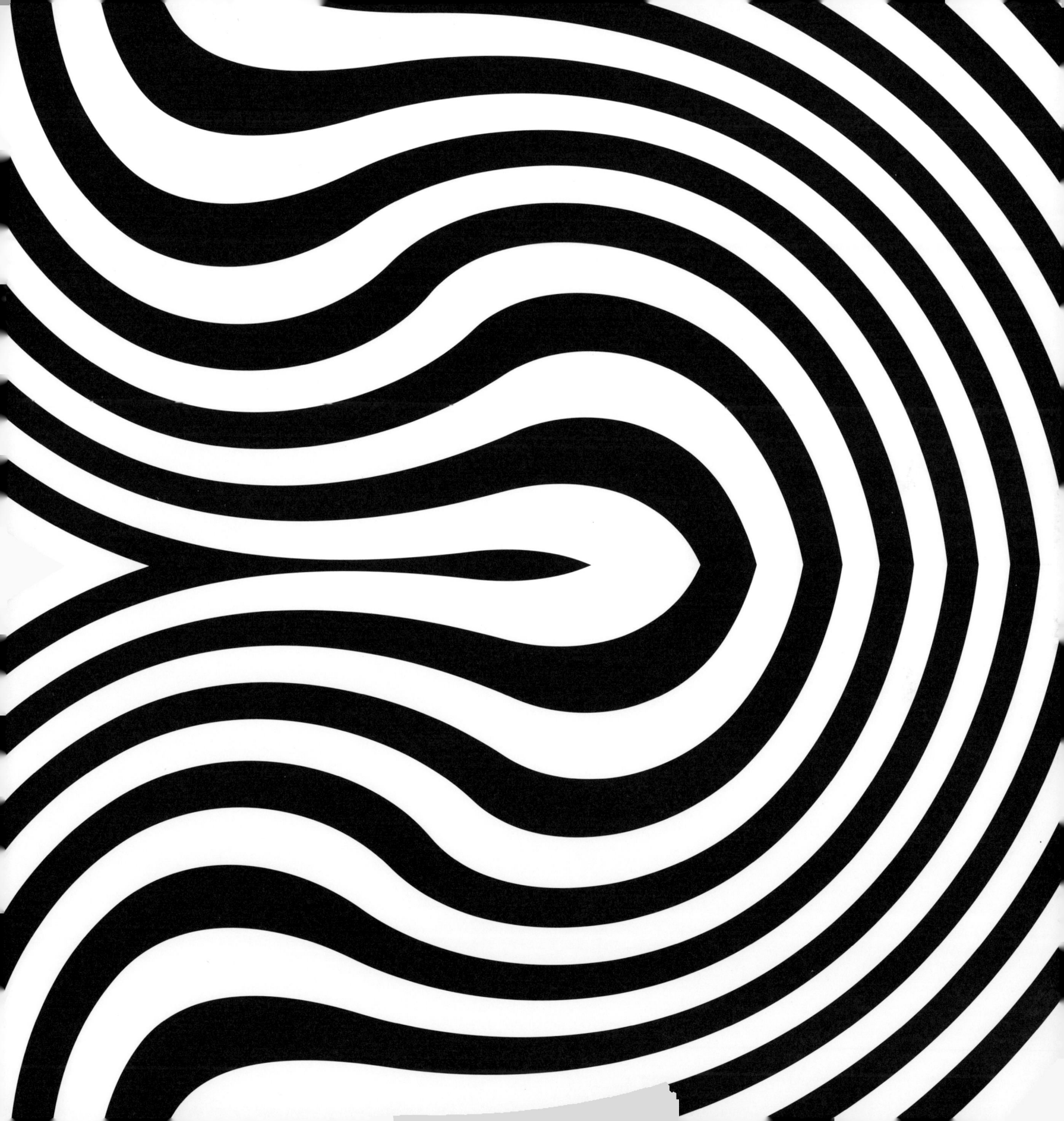

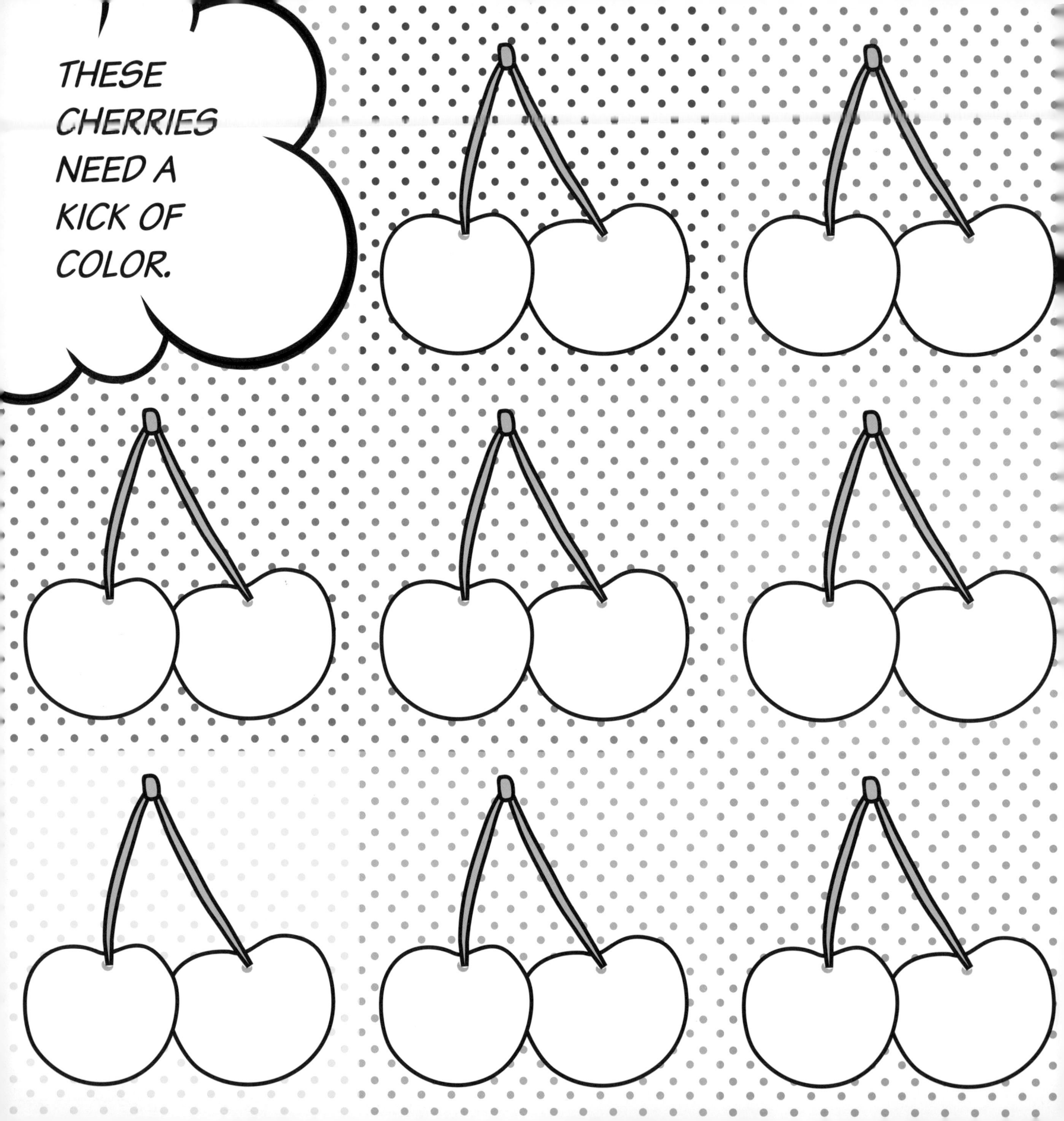
THESE CHERRIES NEED A KICK OF COLOR.

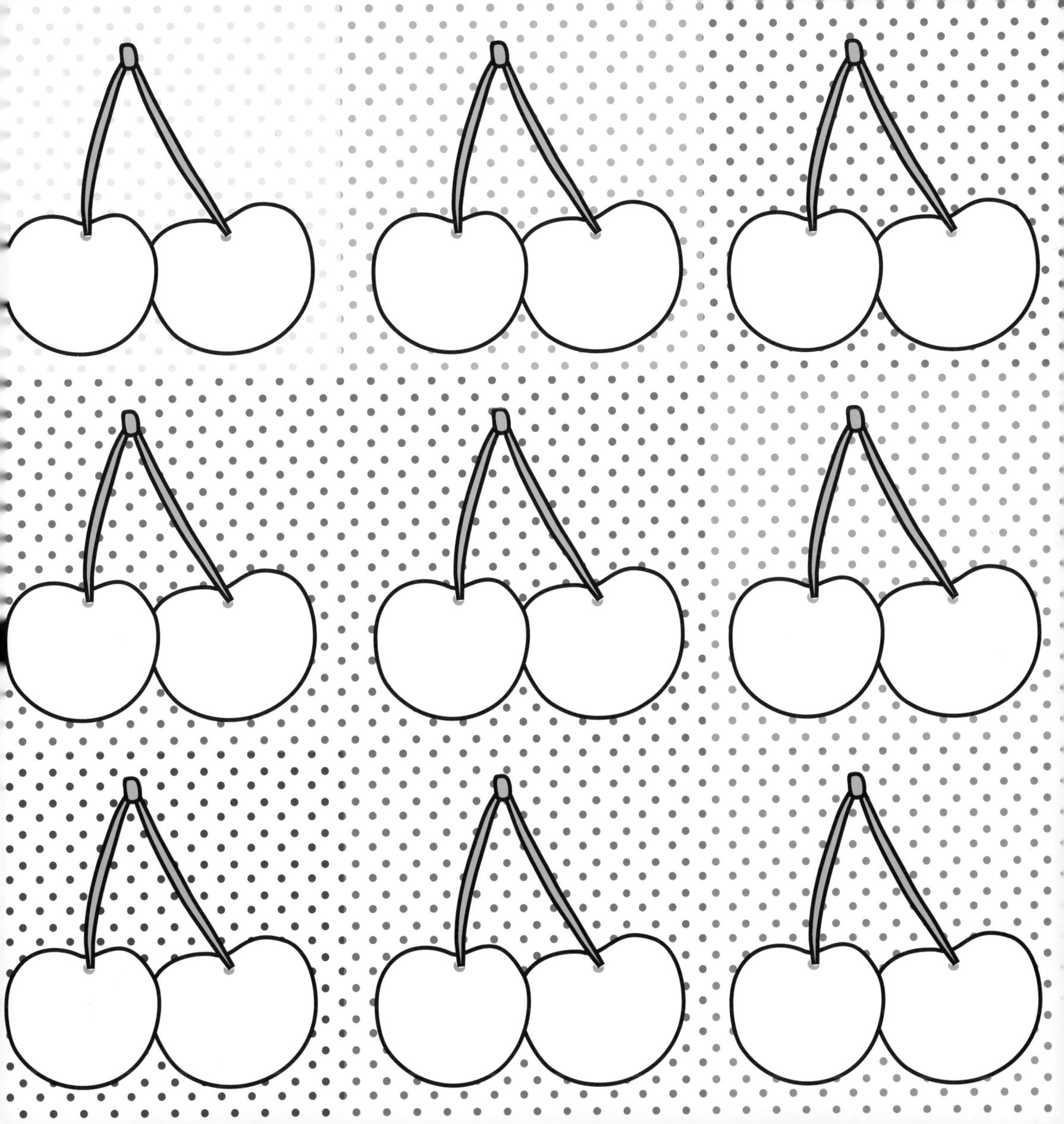

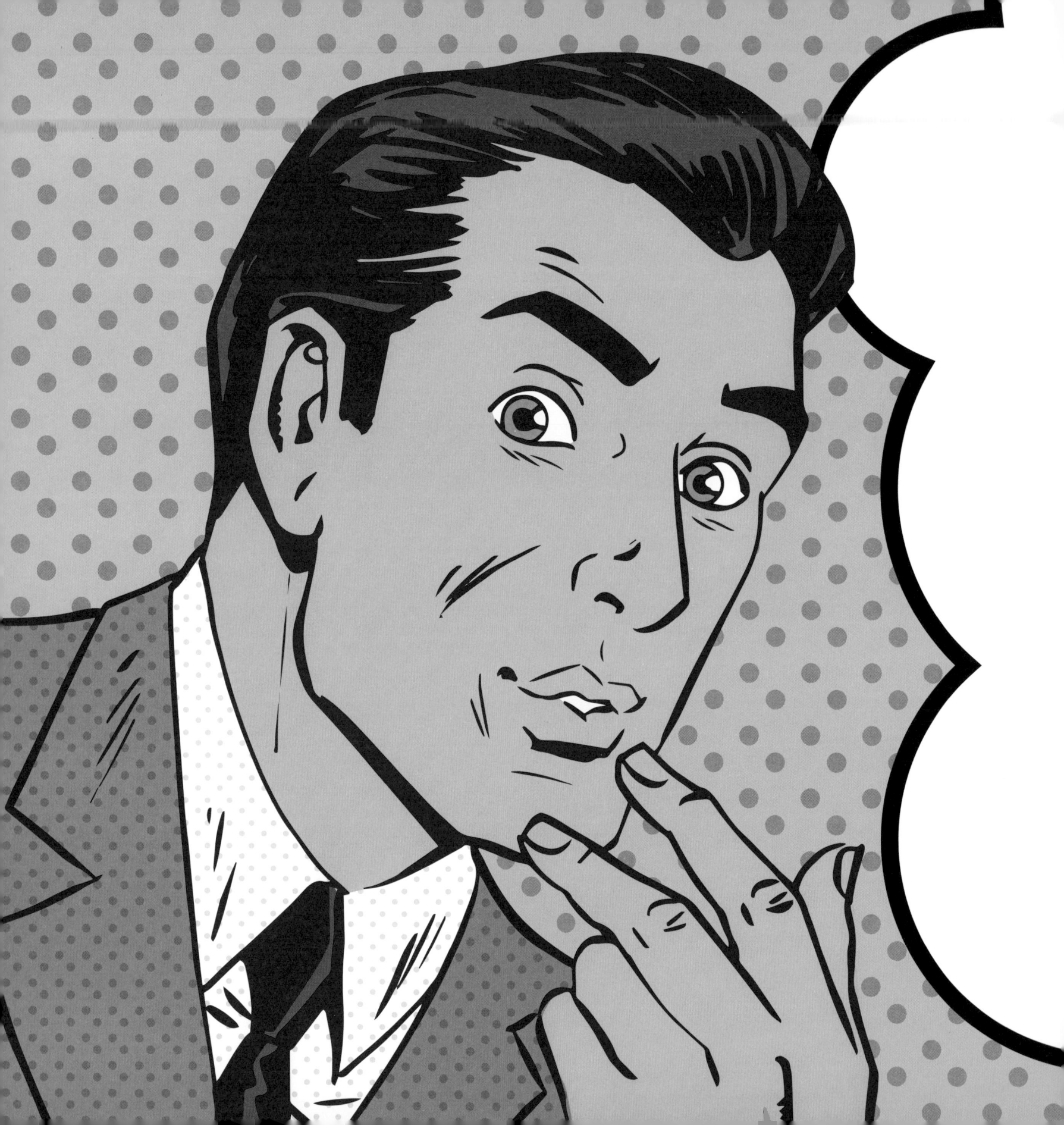

HEY THERE, CUTIE!
DRAW WHAT OR WHO HAS CAUGHT THIS GUY'S EYE.

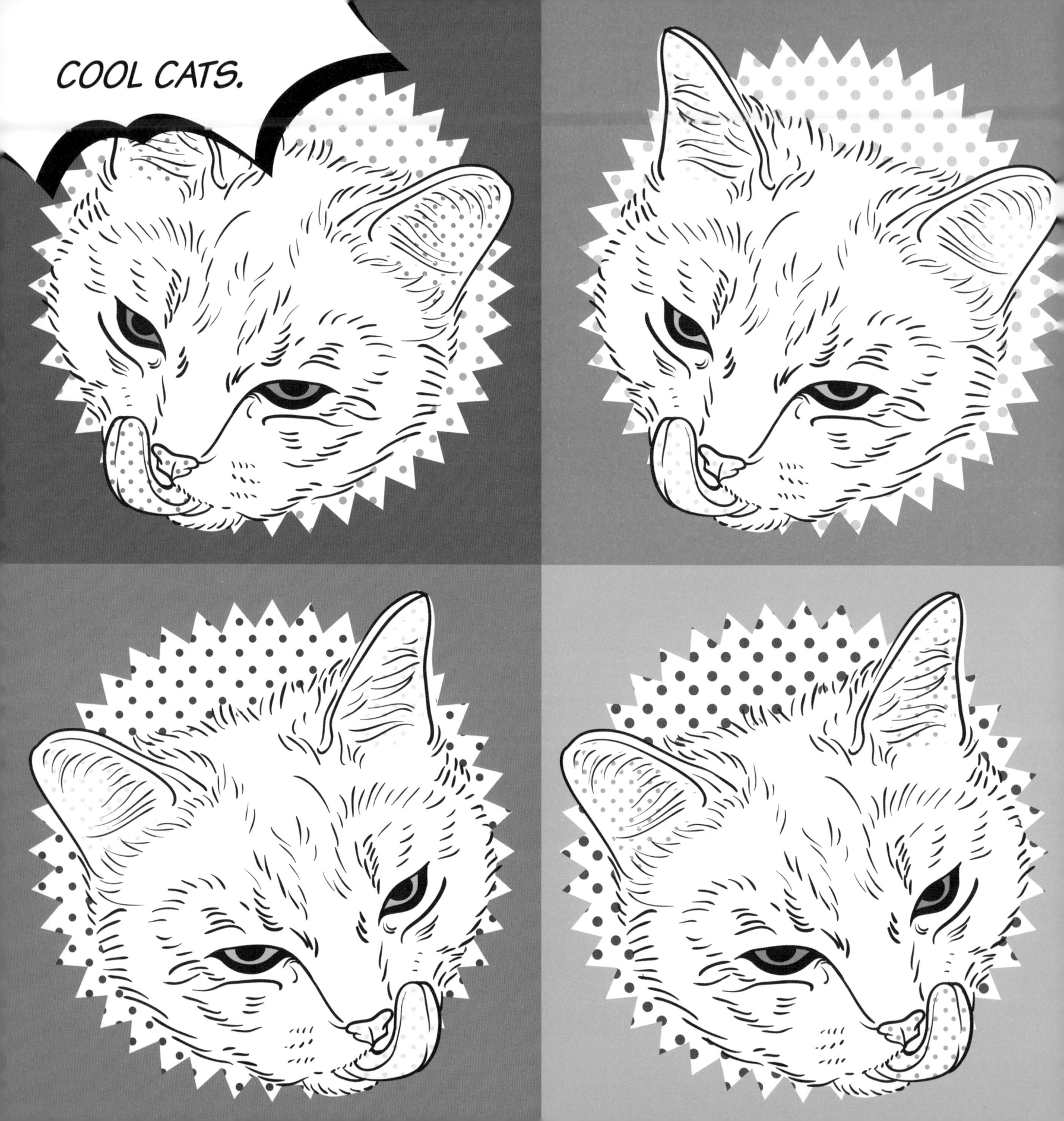
COOL CATS.

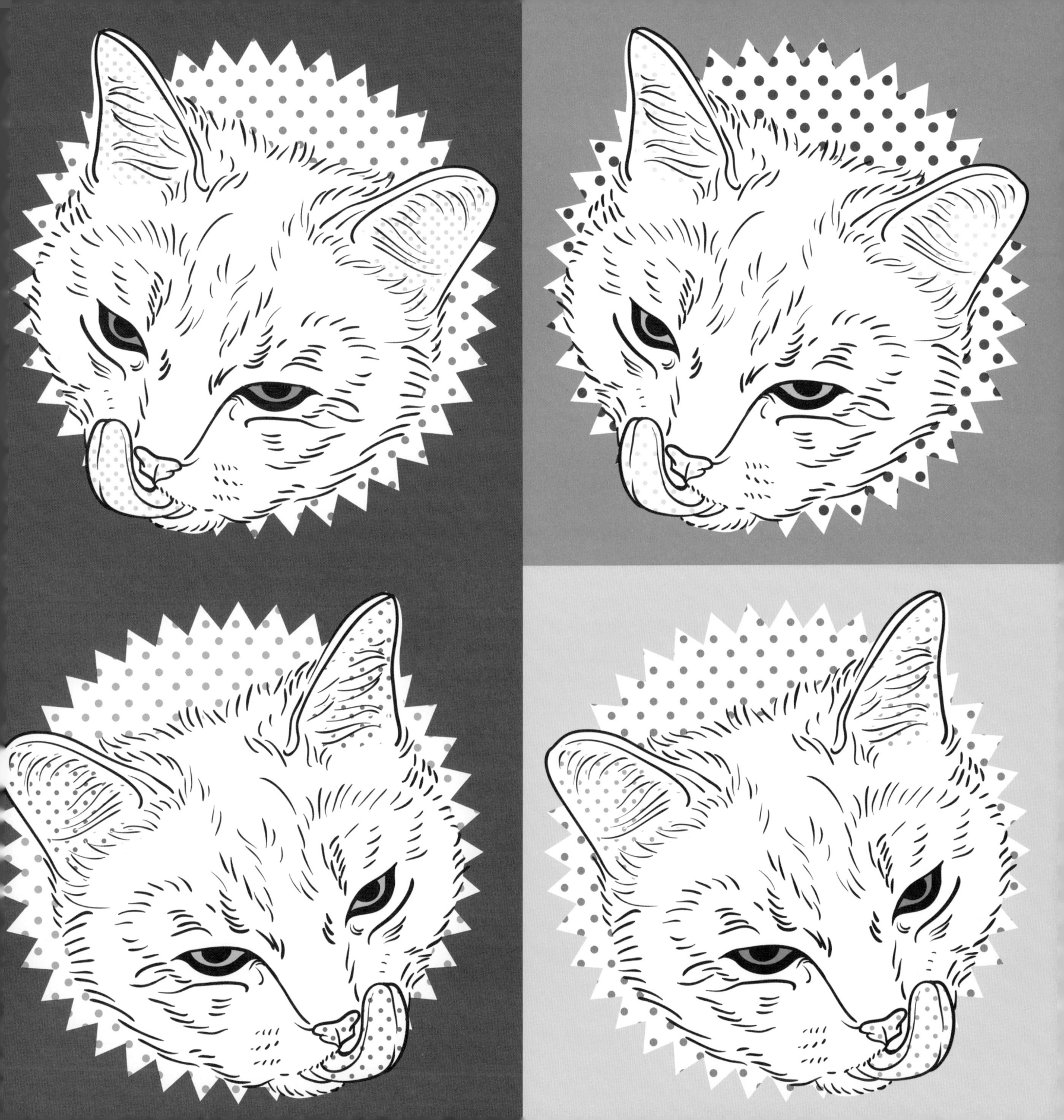

HE LOVES ME? HE LOVES ME NOT? WHAT SECRET SURPRISE AWAITS THIS LOVESICK GAL?

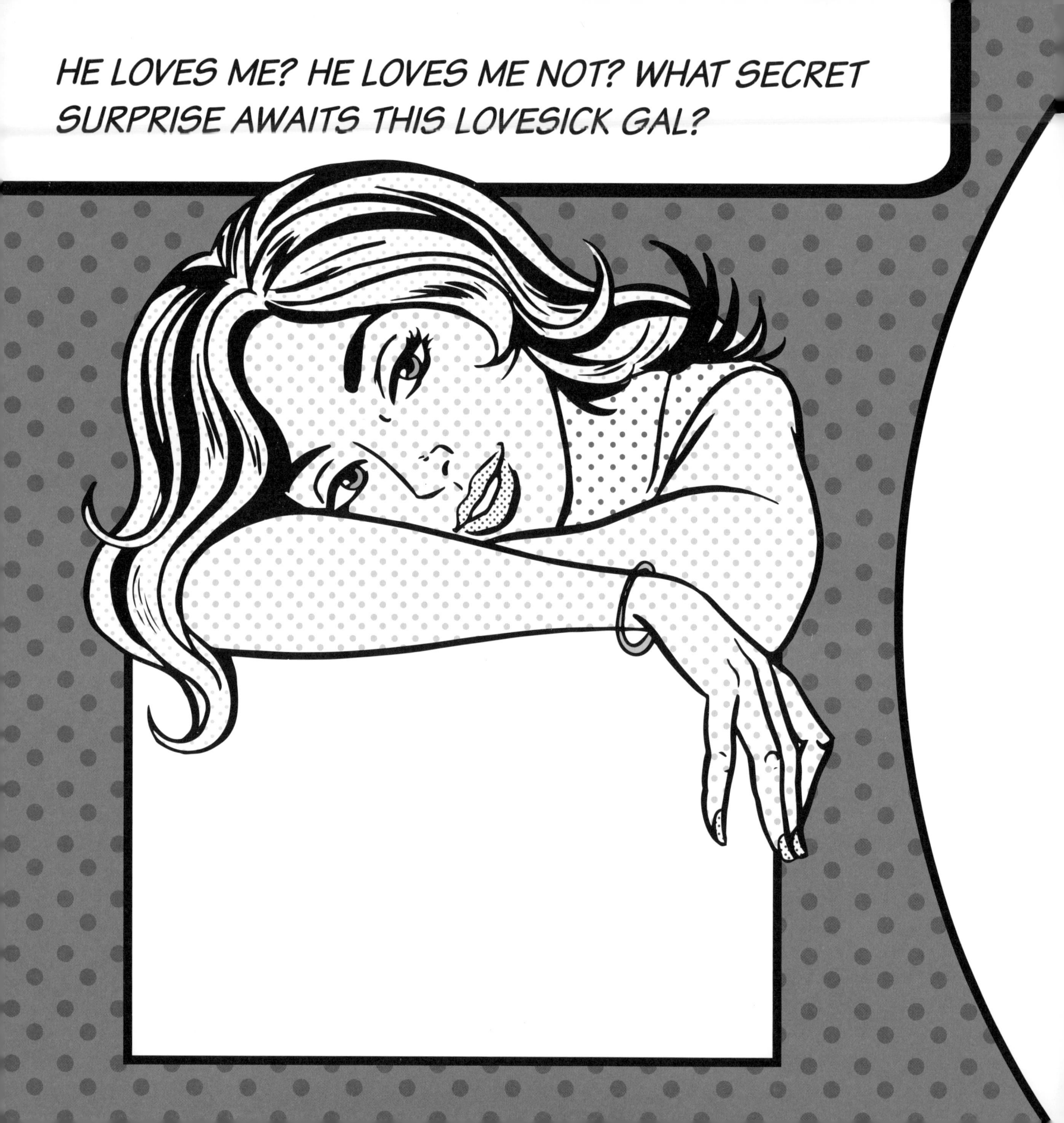

PRINCE CHARMING HAS ARRIVED!

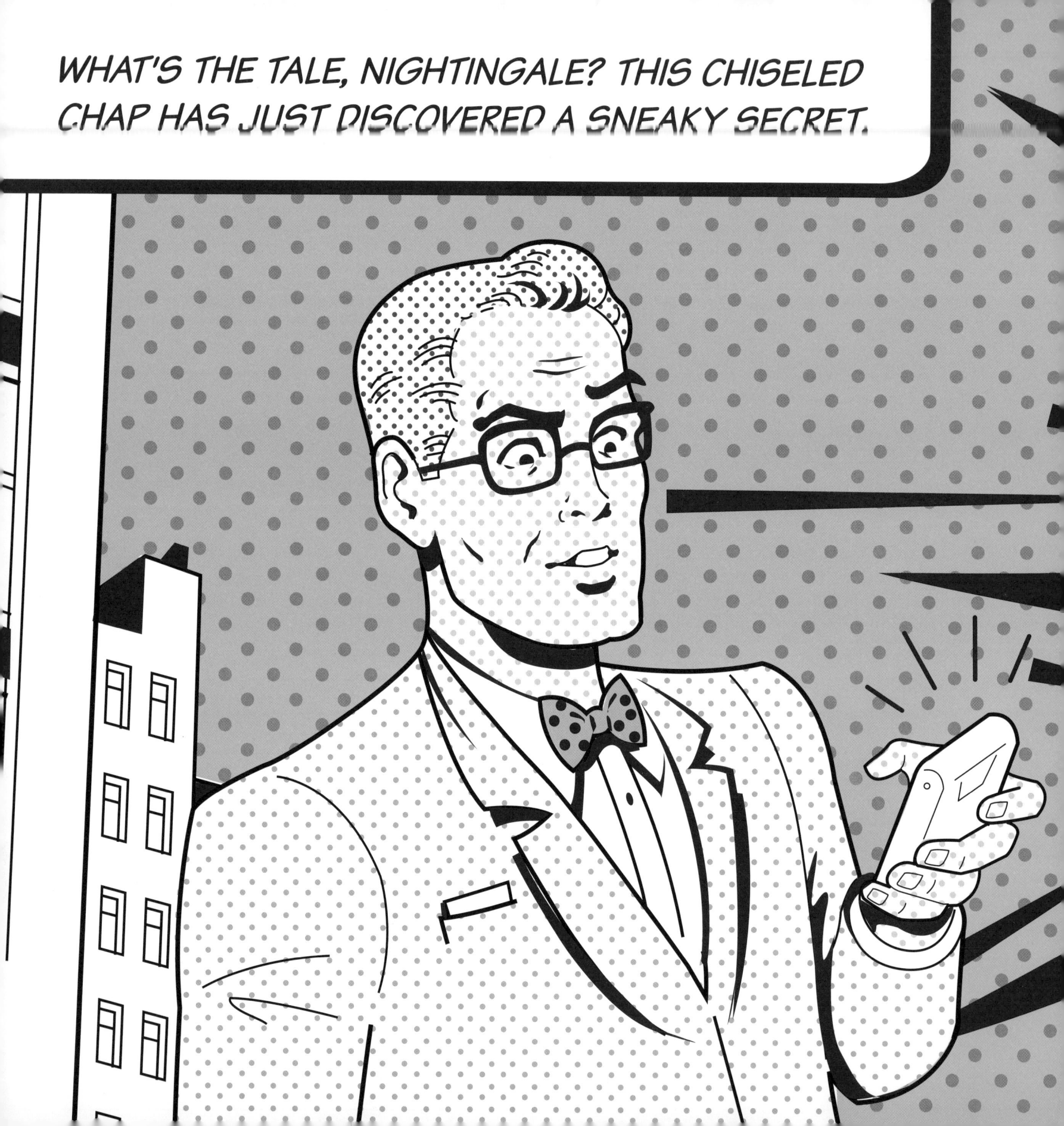
WHAT'S THE TALE, NIGHTINGALE? THIS CHISELED CHAP HAS JUST DISCOVERED A SNEAKY SECRET.

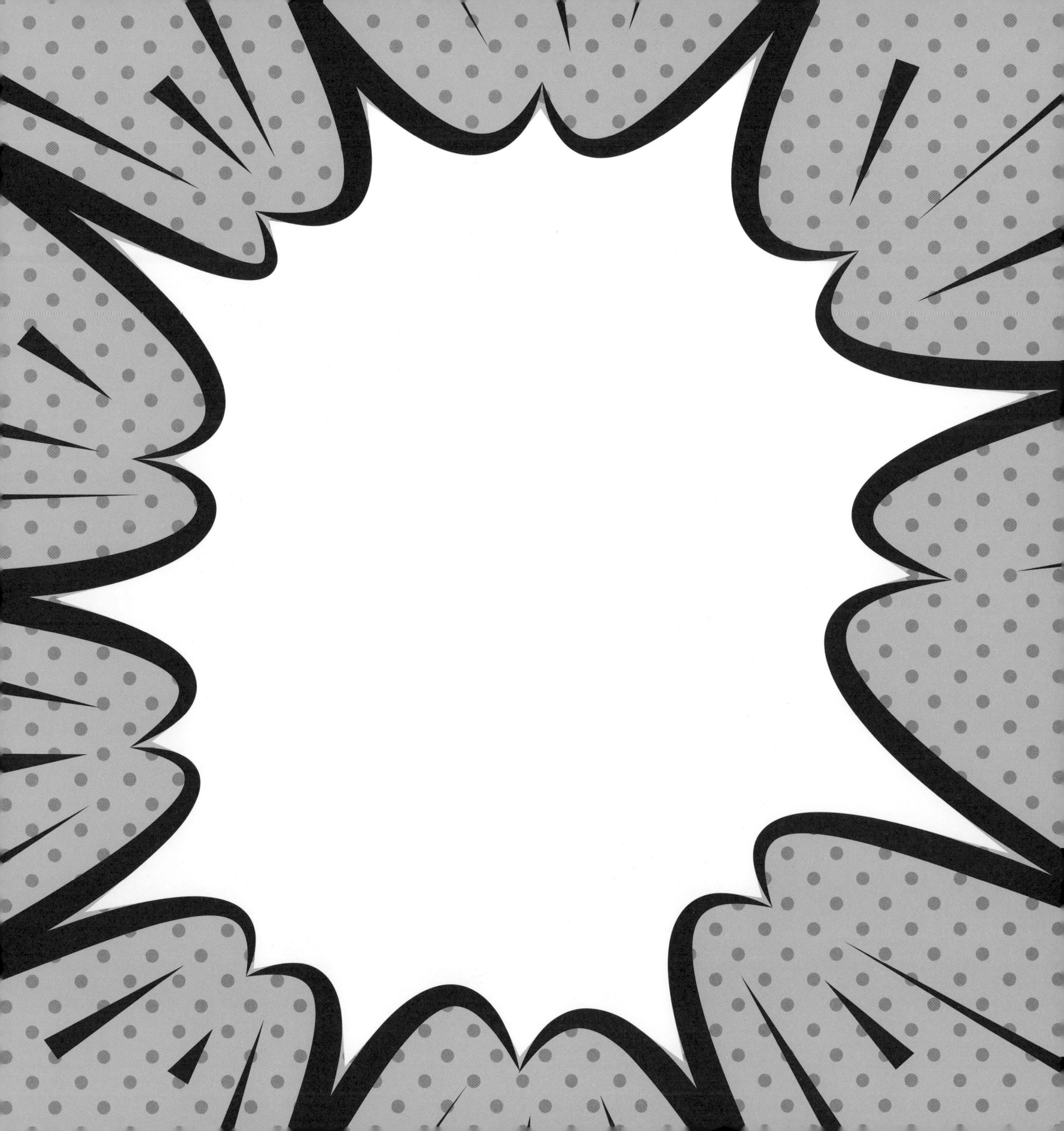

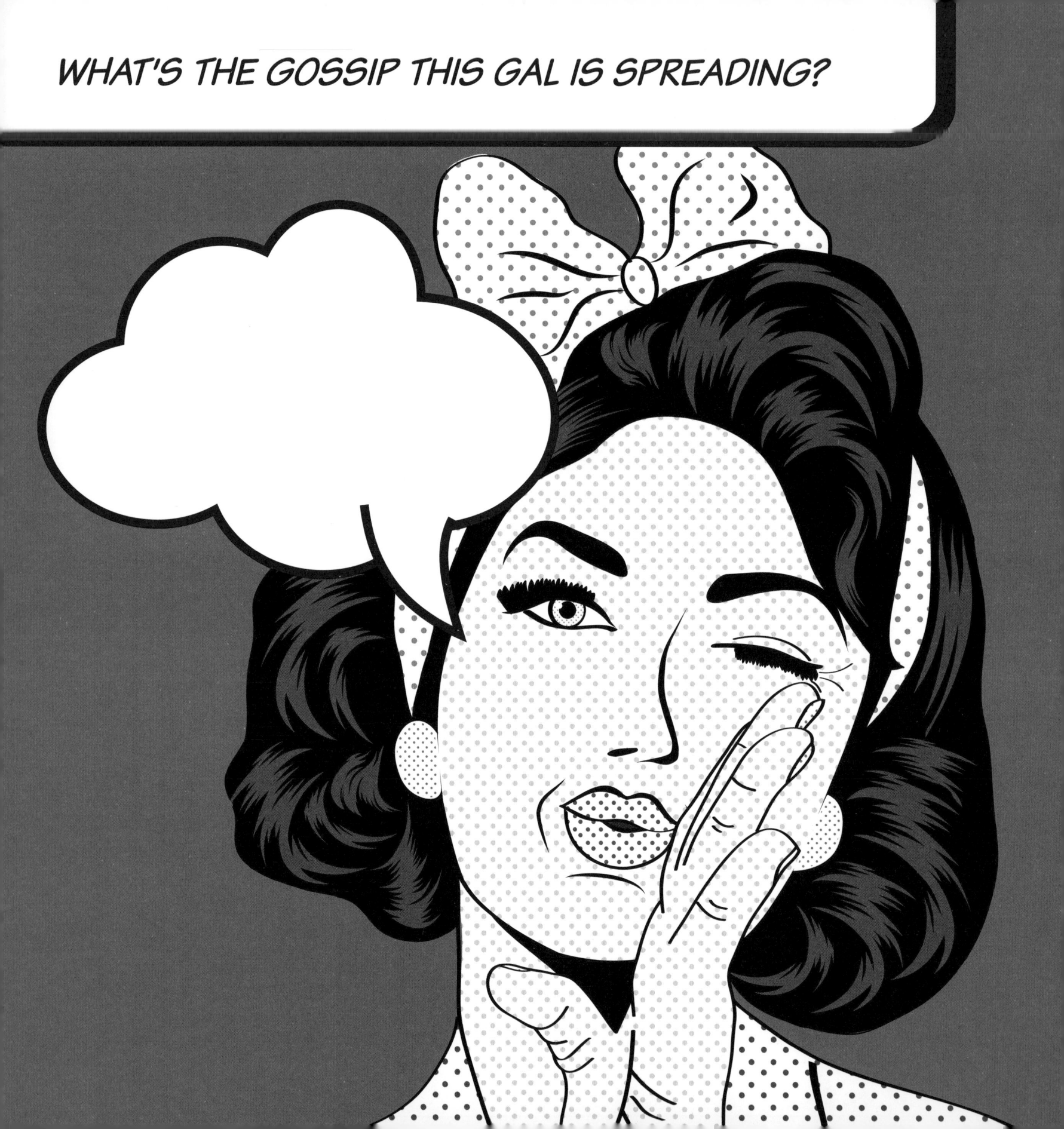
WHAT'S THE GOSSIP THIS GAL IS SPREADING?